Ride in Paradise

The Healing Power in Serving Others

BRAD BEHLE

This book is dedicated to my family.

To Mom and Dad:
Thank you for everything.

To my kids:
I love you. You can accomplish anything you
want if you put your heart and mind to it,
work hard and help others along the way.

To Jena:
You are one of God's angels. Thank you for never doubting
me and for giving me time. Time with you, time for my
pursuits, time to heal and most recently time with my
passing father. I'll forever love you, time and time again.

1

*"All journeys have secret destinations of which
the traveler is unaware."—Martin Buber*

NOVEMBER 2013

I had ridden down this road probably a hundred times
before, only this time was different. I turned off of
Redwood and onto Pioneer Crossing in Saratoga Springs,
Utah. My mind was racing. I was confused about what I was
doing and where I was heading, yet in my heart, I felt that
my destination was inspired.

As I rode my Harley down the street, a feeling of
complete calmness came over me. For the first time in a
while, I knew I was going in the right direction. There was
a peace surrounding me, one that had been familiar to me in
the past, but which had been absent for several years now.
But this time was different. This feeling was unlike any other
I had ever felt before. It was more pure than anything I had
previously experienced.

I was riding solo that day, but I knew for certain that I wasn't alone.

It was cold outside. I had on my leathers; still, the brisk late November air was especially chilly on my face. I had a decently long beard that I decided to grow out for the winter but was now wishing it was even longer in order to protect my face from the bitterness of the coming winter wind.

I was on my way to visit a family, one that I had never met and had only recently learned of the day before.

What was the purpose of me riding over to their house on my Harley in the cold weather? At the time I didn't know the answer. I just knew that sometimes when you feel a strong urge to do a certain thing, especially when it feels like it's coming from someone or something bigger than yourself, you should probably go do it.

Cruising down the street, I wasn't really paying attention to the cold anymore. My mind was elsewhere, thinking of the things that have pushed me away for a while now, things that I have kept hidden deep down inside. I started to ponder a word that has had a profound effect on me for the last ten years. What truly does the word *paradise* even mean? Is it a real place or just an imaginary location we made up to give us hope when we need a break from life?

If you look up the definition, you'll see it's "a state of bliss, pure happiness or delight."

Each individual might have their own idea of what it is. Maybe to some it's the place you go after passing from this life and onto the next, a place where you are reunited with your creator and loved ones.

It could be a favorite place here on earth. One you can go to escape from all of your troubles and to gain some clarity away from the clutter of life. We all have our own image of what our personal paradise is.

To me, it's not one place in particular. It can be anywhere that you can find that blissful moment of pure happiness.

I often find this place when I'm on my motorcycle. I certainly found it riding on this particular cold day.

I think most motorcycle riders experience some form or another of this feeling, it's probably the reason we even keep riding. I know what I felt on my way to visit this family was like nothing I had ever felt before—it was more intense. I didn't want the feeling to leave. It was incredible.

The wind on your face, the hyper awareness of everything that surrounds you, the sound of rumbling pipes that brings a sense of freedom enjoyed on the open road. It's an escape from your worries in the world and your only focus is this awesome moment of you, your bike, and the pavement. Things seem perfect.

An old biker friend of mine would often say when he was out riding that he was in no hurry to get anywhere, because he was already everywhere, he wanted to be. What a great way to look at things. Truly just living in the moment. Not worrying about yesterday or tomorrow. Enjoying now.

In all the years I've been riding, I find this to be true. It is very therapeutic and relaxing after a stressful day. I also enjoy the camaraderie with other bikers; there's an acceptance of all. When you're on a bike, you're part of a family now. Of course, there can be a little beef with some riders depending on the kind of bike you're on. A road bike, sport bike, foreign or American. What matters to me, though, is just that you're out riding.

Have you ever noticed as we pass each other going in the opposite direction, we hold out our left hand? It's a universal wave, a sign of respect to the other person, a way to tell the other to enjoy the ride.

I've found that the general population of people that ride to be some of the coolest, most caring people I know. Most might look like a rough crowd, but appearance isn't everything. Take notice that the next time you see a large group of bikes. If they're not off riding for a good cause, then they're just out enjoying the day, not causing any trouble and just capturing the freedom of the open road.

When I first started riding years ago, I had a 50cc motor scooter. I always loved when a "real biker" on a loud hog would pass and give me the wave. Some wouldn't though, they laughed at scooters. I always respected the ones that would.

My uncle Scott got me interested in bikes and pretty much taught me how to ride. In fact, the day he bought his first Harley, a cherried out Fatboy, I drove him there to pick it up so he could ride it home. Ever since that day, hearing him fire it up for the first time and hearing that heart-pumping rumble, I knew I needed one.

I ended up buying a 1997 Harley Sportster a few months later and for the last 14 years I have ridden thousands of miles and dumped a lot of money into it. I've customized just about everything you can to make it my own. I've souped up the motor giving it more power, put on some tall ape hanger handlebars and added a suicide shift on it that makes some of the most experienced bikers hesitant to take it for a spin. About seven or eight years ago, it was featured in a booth at the Utah Autorama car show.

I've spent a lot of time at local shops learning about how these machines worked so I could wrench on it myself. It's a cool culture to be a part of and allows me to keep a little fire lit on the rebellious side I have (and think we all do).

With riding being such a large part of my adult life up to this point, I was lucky enough to find the right girl to marry, because I have several friends who no longer ride or would love to start, but their wives don't like the idea. Mine loves it.

Jena and I had been dating about a month and had seen each other daily before she even knew I had a bike. I really liked her and was trying to find out where she stood when it came to motorcycles. Was she one that hated them or one that would want to get on the back and go cruise with me? It might seem funny that I put so much thought into this as I went on dates, but the truth is, it mattered to me. I really liked this girl, though, and I didn't want to send her packing if I found out she didn't like motorcycles. I wondered how she would react when she found out how obsessed I was and what a huge part of my life bikes are.

One night, we were out with my childhood best friend Tony and his girlfriend, now wife, Heidi. Jena mentioned a Neal Young song about riding a Harley Davidson and how she dreamed that after retirement she and her husband would take off and tour the country on their bike.

Tony looked at her and said, "That's an awesome plan. What do you think of Brad's Harley?"

She looked at me, both shocked that I had one and mad that I hadn't taken her on a ride yet. Right then, I knew even more to hang on to this one. She could share in my obsession and if things worked out, we could possibly take the retirement tour around the country that she talked about.

Now that we're married, we love to hit the road together. She even has an old 1978 Honda CB125 she's learning to ride on. She enjoys being on the back of mine and one of our favorite things to do is our annual ride up a Utah canyon with Uncle Scott and Aunt Carlene. We always stop for dinner at our favorite spot and listen to some live music being played on the outdoor patio.

As the years have passed, it's been harder for Jena and me to take off together like we used to when we were first married. With two young kids at home, our priorities and free time have changed. Now with Jena pregnant with our third child, we won't be going out on the bike together for a while.

I've considered selling the bike several times and using the money to buy something a little more family friendly. One spring a while back, I actually listed it for sale.

Jena talked me out of it and told me to take down the ad. She knew I'd regret it later. She knows me well, and like I said, she's a keeper!

Back to that cold November day, riding down the road to visit this family, I thought about these memories and many others that have been created on my bike throughout the years. I also sensed a new memory was being made, one that would stay with me for a long time.

I looked up the directions to their house before leaving, so I knew how to get there, but I still wasn't really sure why I felt so strongly that I needed to go.

Hanging from the bottom of my bike is my guardian angel bell. My mom had given it to me years ago as a protector. It's always nice to think you're being watched over as you ride, and more than ever, this day I knew that I was.

Something was guiding me to go there. That something felt as real as the blue sky above me and the black pavement below my tires. I felt like I wasn't alone. It was a great feeling, one that I will never forget.

2

*"Dreams are illustrations from the book your
soul is writing about you."—Marsha Norman*

It was just past 2 p.m. My kids Bode and Solee were now
down for their afternoon naps. I was waiting for my
youngest brother Tyler to come over so we could get in a
quick workout during his lunch break from work. I've turned
a room in my basement into a little gym with kettlebells,
ropes, large tires, TRX trainers and other fun unconventional
fitness equipment that I use with my clients.

I'm a fitness trainer and work early mornings at a
studio and outdoor parks. Whatever we're using for the day,
I grab from my basement and load up in the car. It makes
it nice and convenient for me because I don't need to travel
far to get in my own personal training session, especially the
couple days a week when Jena is on shift as a registered nurse
and I'm home with the kids after my morning classes.

When Ty showed up, we went downstairs and started
warming up by getting our blood flowing and ready to work
out. After about five minutes, I still couldn't get into it. My

mind was somewhere else. No matter how hard I tried to focus, I couldn't. I needed to take care of something and asked Ty if he would stay with the sleeping kids, get in his workout while I took off for a short while. He was fine with it but needed to get back to work shortly.

Part of my lack of focus was due to not sleeping well the night before. I was tired and dragging and had tossed and turned all night long. My mind wandered rapidly; I couldn't shut it off. I glanced at the clock showing 2:30 a.m. and knew my 4:30 a.m. alarm was going to be brutal.

My mind had been on a conversation I had earlier in the day before trying to sleep. While browsing some online classifieds looking for my next project to fix and flip for a profit, I found a classic MasterCraft Stars and Stripes ski boat. It looked really nice; especially considering it was over twenty-five years old.

It didn't seem to need much work done and looked to be in pristine condition. I hadn't really considered buying a boat just to store for the wintertime since it was now November but decided to call on it anyway and see if he was set on the price. Maybe I could talk him down, use it next spring and summer and then sell it?

We live out by Utah Lake and are only a mile from the local marina. My four-year-old and two-year-old kids are constantly reminding me how badly they want another boat since we sold our last one. We love boating, wakeboarding and wakesurfing as a family. Even though my kids are still young, it's a great activity to do together that we really enjoy. It's one of the main reasons we moved out by the lake. We also love to paddleboard and anything else that gets us out on the water.

I dialed the number on the classified ad and the owner answered. I started asking questions about how it ran, if it needed any work and why he was selling it?

"Runs great," he said, nothing wrong that he knew of and they were selling it because they didn't take it out much this past summer.

He told me that they had owned it over ten years and he hates to get rid of it, but he and his wife probably wouldn't be able to bring themselves to head out to the lake for a long time.

"Why is that?" I asked. "Are you guys too busy or just not into boating anymore?"

"Well," he said softly, "this past June my extended family was involved in a boating accident at Lake Powell. Not in this boat, another one. It's tragic. My five-year-old little brother-in-law died."

He then said how much they loved to go boating but knew how hard it would be on the family to go out on any lake right now.

That is horrible, I thought to myself, that poor family having to go through something as tragic as this.

I told him I was sorry for their loss and hoped they would be able to find some kind of peace. I appreciated him telling me the story even though it probably wasn't the best sales pitch for a potential buyer, but I could appreciate his honesty and desire in wanting to sell it.

I didn't know at the time that there was another reason that I picked up the phone to call. It actually had nothing to do with his boat, but rather everything to do with what he had just told me.

After hanging up with him, I started thinking a lot about his family and the little boy. I thought about the pain his parents must be dealing with. I looked up the accident online and found the boys name was Keaton. I actually recalled hearing about it earlier that summer right after it had happened. It seemed more personal now that I had talked to a family member about it.

It was late November and a week from Thanksgiving. It had been around five months since the accident happened, and with the holidays approaching, I imagined the pain this family must be enduring. My son is only a year younger than Keaton and I couldn't fathom going through something like this with one of my own kids.

It was another reminder of how truly precious life is and prompted me to hold them a lot closer that night as we put them down for bed.

We're always on the move in our society and sometimes it's really nice to just slow down and pay attention to what truly matters.

This day, I slowed down a lot. I pondered a lot. That phone call had me thinking differently than I had been before I dialed that number.

Was I taking full advantage of each day? Did my family know how much I loved them?

I tell my kids each night as I put them down to bed that they can accomplish anything they want in life as long as they put their heart and mind to it, work hard and help other people along the way. Was I being a hypocrite when I told them this? Did I believe it, and was I living up to it?

"Where could I do better?" I kept asking myself.

I appreciate these life reminders. They help keep me grounded on the important matters. They bring me back to what we went through as a family nearly ten years ago with my older brother Jason and how you never know what day could be your last.

I think back on all of the help we received from so many people after he died and how I should strive harder to return the kindness and serve others more often. Life passes quickly; I need to live each day with a more committed purpose.

I typically have no problem falling asleep. In fact, Jena says it's a talent, both how fast I can fall asleep and the random places I can shut my eyes and be out cold. My son got this from me. We can pass out into dreamland at the snap of a finger. Not that particular night though. I tried for hours.

Each time I closed my eyes, I saw little Keaton. Even though I had never met him, I saw his picture from the online obituary. I thought of his sweet family as well. My heart ached for them.

Why had I called on that boat? What caused this family's situation to affect me so strongly? Accidents take place every day where someone unfortunately loses their life. Why is this one any different when I didn't even know them personally? After several hours of these thoughts and not sleeping, I felt restless and tired.

Call it a dream, inspiration, divine intervention or just plain lack of sleep, almost instantly I had a feeling come over me. It was peaceful. I was no longer restless but feeling really calm. I was now wide awake. I remember wondering, was this a dream and had I finally fallen asleep?

I wasn't sure. I'm not an expert on how the mind works; I just knew I was feeling something strongly. It was like I was being told to do something by someone very familiar. Without knowing why, I felt encouraged to get out of bed and go upstairs into my office. As I got up and started walking, I knew it wasn't a dream.

It had been nearly ten years since my brother Jason had died and for the first time in a long time, I was feeling really close to him.

I tried not to wake my sleeping family as I headed upstairs. I went into the office and immediately opened the bottom desk drawer. Inside, right on top, I found some important keepsakes that I haven't looked at in years.

The first thing I pulled out was a newspaper clipping of an article from nearly nine years ago.

The title reads: **Ride In Paradise** charity generates money for kids, honors the memory of Jason Behle."

The article took place back in 2005, almost a year to the day from when my older brother had passed away.

We organized a charity motorcycle ride and raised money for a local children's charity in honor of his two young kids, Mykell and Luke. It was a great experience and a way for us to give back after receiving so much love and support from so many friends and people we didn't even know. The last several months I had been contemplating whether to organize another ride to recognize the ten years mark of his passing.

Well, here it was, 2 a.m., just a couple of hours before I needed to get up for work, and I'm sitting in my office reading over this article again and again.

I had tears streaming down my face. It's as though my brother was telling me something. I wasn't sure what it was or if I had gone crazy, I just felt strongly that I needed to go do something.

3

"As I lay rubber down the street, I pray for traction I can keep, but if I spin and begin to slide, please dear God, protect my sweet ride!"
—Funny biker's prayer

I remember it like it was yesterday when my older brother Jason got his own bike. It was a nice spring afternoon in 2004. He rode it over to my parents' house from Tooele, Utah.

His father-in-law had just given it to him, and he couldn't wait to come over and show us. He was so excited. Sure, it was old, a little beat up and wasn't a Harley, but we planned to punch out the baffles in the muffler to make it sound more like one. But most importantly, we could finally go ride together now.

It was a big bagger type bike, which would be nice and comfortable for the longer trips. I was excited he finally got one and couldn't wait to go out and cruise with him.

He hung around for a little before he decided to go. It was typical for us Behle brothers to cause some trouble messing around, and this day was no different. I wanted to do a big burnout and get the tires smoking, so I put my bike up against the curb, held down the front brake, and let out the clutch while giving it gas. It was awesome, smoke blowing everywhere, the motor revving loudly as we laughed, and I thought I was so hardcore.

Just then I accidentally let off on the brake slightly causing it to jump up the curb while dragging me to the side as it headed towards the very fence Jason had built years before. I knew I couldn't let go or it would bust straight through, knocking the whole thing over and even worse, possibly damaging my sweet ride.

Luckily, I barely stopped it inches before crashing through and was able to keep from laying it down on the grass. I looked at Jason in shock at what had just happened. He told me I was an idiot and we burst out laughing at the situation and my carelessness.

It was time for him to go, so he said he'd see us all later, and loaded up on his bike to leave. I decided I'd ride part of the way back with him; it would be our first time riding together with his new cruiser. We had talked about this for a while and now he finally had a bike. It was reality and it was happening.

He took off, waving goodbye to the family, and I followed close behind. We stopped at a red light and he turned to me and said, "Man, you're living the life; your Harley is so awesome!"

I chuckled as I thought to myself, "Yeah, it is. My life is good."

Truth is though, I was in my early twenties and still living with my parents. Girls seemed to like the bad boy image I portrayed, but the living at home thing wasn't all that impressive.

After returning from a two-year church service mission in Paraguay, I had decided to continue living with them and go to a local community college rather than move away for school. I figured I had just gained the experience of living away in a different country; and this way I could save some money and get through my general education requirements without getting into student loan debt. After finishing my general education, I could then decide where to go afterward.

It was a good plan. All except for telling my dates I still lived with my mom and dad part. That still wasn't impressive.

The funny thing about my brother telling me I was the lucky one, I actually thought the same thing about him. He was living the good life, married to a pretty girl, had two great young kids and a nice house of his own.

You know the saying; the grass is always greener… He thought I was living a life with few worries, and with enough money for toys and my minimal responsibilities, but the truth was I knew someday I would want what he had. He was the one "living the life."

There are five of us kids in the family. Jason was the oldest and I'm the second and only two years behind him. Like most brothers close in age, we were either the best of friends or worst of enemies. We played sports together, caused lots of trouble, fought with one another and did everything else close brothers do. I imagine we're a large part of why my dad's hair went gray while he was still in his thirties.

In school, his friends would always call me little Behle, which I found funny because I was the bigger and taller one. He took the role of the older brother seriously, always seeing that I was taken care of. I think he wanted to protect me from making some of the same mistakes he had made, a "do as I say, not as I do" type of thing. He was always watching out for me.

I learned a lot from him in High School, mainly what not to do. He had quite the reputation and I would often be asked if I was fun and crazy like he was. I liked to goof around, but I took sports more seriously and he took being a party animal a little more seriously.

I still laugh thinking back to the time we drove to school in his 4x4 Ford Ranger one cold winter morning. I was a sophomore and didn't have my driver's license, so I'd hitch a ride with him to school. He would usually drop me off and then head to breakfast for the first couple of class periods before making it there himself.

This is one of the many reasons my mom wasn't sure he was actually going to graduate until they called his name and she saw him walking down the aisle to get his diploma.

On this particular drive to school I remember it being cold, I flipped on the truck heater to warm up the cab, just to have him shut it right back off.

"It's busted, I need to fix it," he said.

"What are you talking about? Seems like it's working fine to me."

I flipped it back on only to have him shut it right back off. After going back and forth a little, he finally confessed why he didn't want it on. He recently had a bag of his buddy's weed that was sitting on the dash spill into the vents as he made a sharp turn.

Every time he turned the heater on, it created a "hotbox" effect and stunk up the truck. He told me he didn't want me to be around that kind of stuff, so we just had to toughen up and drive in the cold truck until he fixed it.

This is one of the many times I can remember him being protective and trying to keep his little brother from making some of the mistakes he felt he had. He was always protective of my siblings and me.

When I first got my Harley, some people would try to discourage me from riding by telling me how dangerous it is. When Jason would hear someone trying to scare me, he'd mention how many car accidents there were versus the number of motorcycle accidents he had worked on.

He was a paramedic for a local hospital and ran on the ambulance crew. He always would stick up for my love of riding even though he had been the first on scene to some very serious motorcycle accidents. I knew the ratio of cars to bikes on the road is a lot higher so obviously there would be more car accidents, plus you typically get injured a lot worse on a bike, so his argument didn't really hold any ground. It felt good having him stick up for me though, and to know that he had my back.

Growing up I didn't like him borrowing any of my stuff. He had a bad habit of not returning things. In fact, about two years ago, I got a call from an old friend of his. He had always felt bad about borrowing my baseball catcher's mitt from Jason and never returning it some twenty years ago. He wanted to replace it all these years later. I thought that was a nice gesture but told him it was fine and to not worry about it.

When we were older, Jason approached me to take my Harley for the weekend. I was understandably hesitant based off his track record of borrowing. It was for a good cause he told me. There was going to be a firefighter/paramedic charity ride and several of his buddies and co-workers were going. I ended up saying no, explaining that I would feel guilty or somehow responsible if he laid it down and got hurt.

I think he could see right through me and knew I was more concerned he'd wreck my bike than I was about him getting injured.

Looking back now, I realize that material stuff isn't important. I actually feel bad I didn't let him take it that day. In fact, it's one of the biggest regrets I have about my brother.

I can imagine how fun it would have been riding with his buddies and co-workers.

I think this is one of the reasons I was so happy he got his own bike. We could ride together, and he wouldn't be begging to use mine anymore.

That first ride with him is one of those moments you don't easily forget. We'd been through a lot together and created a ton of memories both good and bad in the last twenty-five years.

We sped down the highway doing 75 mph side by side, rubber on the road and wind in our hair. Nothing else mattered.

We looked over at each other grinning from ear to ear. A perfect moment, the image is forever etched in my mind.

Our first ride together… would also become our last.

4

"Death is not the greatest loss in life. The greatest loss is what dies inside us while we live."—Norman Cousins

Summer was in full swing on the day of July 6, 2004. It was a hot Utah desert day. My dad was the construction manager of some extremely high-end rooftop condominiums being built in downtown Salt Lake City. They were almost finished and the landscaping was being installed, including some sprinkler drip lines for the flowerbeds to conserve on water.

At the time, I worked for my uncle Scott and his property management company. We were in charge of the landscaping needs there. With all the work to be done, my dad and Scott had coordinated to have all of the Behle boys up and working together.

My younger brothers, Mike and Ty were busy planting some flowers in beds that didn't need drip irrigation lines and already had enough sprinkler head coverage. I was adjusting different sprinkler heads making sure they were hitting all the sod and planter beds and leaving the ones that needed a drip system for Jason to install. He was the sprinkler specialist and was going to come up later after waking—he had been on the late shift on the ambulance the night before.

An entrepreneur at a young age, he always did something in addition to his main job in the medical field.

At the time he had a small sprinkler installation and repair business as well as his full-time job working as a surveyor for an environmental company. On top of this and his family life, he still found time to work in what he truly loved: as a medic on the ambulance crew for the hospital in the city he lived in.

I learned a lot from him about landscaping and irrigation. This helped me when I decided to start my own landscape maintenance company later down the road that I ended up selling before starting my fitness business.

My brother helped a lot of people. It's hard to know how many neighbors and friends he installed sprinkler systems for. Often each summer time he could be found digging or installing sprinkler pipe for someone. In fact, I remember the girl I was dating at the time had just returned home from a break from school. Her dad was doing the landscaping for their new home. Me talking a big game and wanting to impress him, volunteered to help install it the next day.

I frantically called my brother that night asking questions on how to do things I had never done before, like hooking up the manifolds and the stop and waste valve. He said not to worry and that he'd drive the hour to her house and help with the tricky parts.

We spent the whole Saturday working on this thing. I thought for sure this would impress her dad and score me some major points with him.

Well, I guess not because when it was time for dinner, he loaded up his family and took them all out to pizza, leaving us behind to finish his job. I was surprised that he didn't offer us anything, especially to go out to dinner with them. I only had a day to spend with her before she headed back to school, and after spending the whole day working, I thought the least he could do was invite me to go with them.

As they left, I remember complaining to Jason and saying that we should just go and leave the rest of the work for him to do on his own.

"We're about done, man, let's just finish it up," he said. "Who cares if he seems grateful or not, at least we did our part helping someone out."

I learned a great lesson that day on unselfishly serving others. I also learned that it was probably time to find another possible future father-in-law to impress.

It was getting really hot on top of the building. Despite the heat, I was excited to hang out with all my brothers and do some work together. I wasn't sure how my dad and uncle thought we would get anything done though— we're infamous for turning anything and everything into a competitive game that almost always ended badly with one of us being a sore loser.

My poor parents; us four boys and our sister sure put them through a lot. Our house was always chaotic with our rowdy bunch, especially when we had friends around. One thing was for sure, we always knew how to have fun; sometimes we just took it a little too far.

We started just after 8 am, and I could tell that it was going to be a scorcher that day. It was already well over 100 degrees Fahrenheit and being on top of the building made it even worse and seem hotter. We had already been there several hours and were getting a little frustrated that Jason hadn't shown up yet. We couldn't finish the job until the drip lines were installed, and this was his responsibility.

My Dad tried to reach him on his cell phone a couple times to see where he was, but he didn't answer. We figured he slept past his alarm after his late-night graveyard shift on the ambulance.

A little while later our world changed forever. My dad was down in his office and received a call from Jason's wife. He ran up and told us that Jason was headed to the hospital and had been found in bed not breathing.

He told me to come with him and we would hurry out to the hospital he was being rushed to.

Panicked thoughts raced through my head, but I pushed them out telling myself that things will be all right. It's just a precautionary thing; his allergies are probably bothering him or something similar and besides…bad stuff happens to other people, not to us. It'll be fine.

We hopped into my dad's Jeep Grand Cherokee that was fast and fun to drive. We got on the freeway headed out to Tooele County and were flying down the road. It's about a forty-minute drive from Salt Lake to Tooele, but we made it there in less than twenty because my dad was speeding, weaving in and out of traffic. I just tried to stay calm and said a silent prayer asking for cars to get the crap out of the way and that we would make it there safely. I also asked that my brother would be watched over and that he would be fine.

I didn't know what to think about the situation. Was it really that serious or were we just being overcautious by speeding out there?

"He's probably just being a drama queen," I said to myself. "I'm sure he's alright."

He didn't really take care of his health, but he was still so young, that despite his unhealthy habits, I didn't really see it being a heart attack or anything of that nature. How serious could the problem be? I had no idea what to expect. I just knew my dad was driving fast!

About five minutes into the drive, my dad answered his phone. It was my brother's wife, Michelle; I could hear her screaming from the other end. I realized maybe it was now more serious than I previously thought.

"Hurry Fred, get out here!" she yelled.

My dad handed me his phone so he could concentrate on driving. I put it to my ear and what I heard next was something I wasn't ready for. I don't think anyone is ever prepared for something like this.

"Brad, he's not breathing, he's not breathing. Please get out here; please…he's not going to make it, he won't make it," she said frantically.

"No!" I said sternly. "Don't say that. Do NOT say that. He'll be fine. We're on our way. We'll be right there. Everything will be fine."

My dad turned on the hazard lights, stepped on the gas pedal even more and drove in the fast lane. He turned on his flashers and honked while I waved my hands out the window trying to get cars to move. It was like a movie where there was a high-speed chase going on and cars were getting out of the way leaving us a wide-open lane.

I usually liked taking the drive out there to his house. When you pass by the south side of the Great Salt Lake with your window down, you almost feel like you're somewhere near the ocean as you smell the salt in the air. This time I don't even recall passing the lake. I remember that my dad's Jeep kept slugging down when we'd hit the governor switch at 110 mph. Despite the speed limiter slowing us down, we still made it out there in record time.

He lived just down the street from the hospital. You'd pass right by it every time you went to his house. I never in a million years thought my first time actually stepping into this place, after years of driving by it, would be for this reason.

They were expecting our arrival and immediately took us to the room where he was. I walked in, but after one glance, I had to look away. The last time I was in the same hospital room with him was ten years earlier. He was driving me to my friend Justin's house for his birthday party and a car turned in front of us at an intersection. We t-boned it hard. I remember waking up next to him in the emergency room after we had been rushed by ambulance. We both crashed through the windshield and were pretty cut up. Being the protector, he was to me, the first thing he says after I wake us is:

"Sorry bro." Even though the accident wasn't his fault, he felt really bad.

Now, as my dad and I walked into the room where he was lying, I wanted badly for him to just sit up and to say something like he did before. I wanted him to say anything, to just acknowledge that we were there.

He had nothing on except a sheet covering his legs and chest. There was a breathing tube stuck down his throat. His face and body were a light blue color.

My dad and I walked up to him and placed our hands-on top of his head. It was cold to the touch. My eyes were closed because I couldn't open them and see him like this. I tried to picture a better situation in my head than what was really happening. It was real though. No matter what I thought, this was reality. Just then I felt a real calmness come over me, I wasn't sure if things would be alright, but at the same time I knew they would be.

In the L.D.S. faith, (Church of Jesus Christ of Latter Day Saints) we believe those worthy and ordained elders can possess the power to act in God's name through blessings or a prayer. We call this power the Priesthood. I've seen it at work many times in my life. I gave and participated in hundreds of blessings while serving as an ordained missionary in South America. My dad was a missionary in Ireland when he was nineteen and has since had many years of using this priesthood power with our family.

At the beginning of each school year, my dad would bless us to be healthy and strong both mentally and physically and that we would work hard during the school year and tap into our best abilities. He gave us blessings of comfort whenever we needed it and when we were sick, he would bless us to feel better. We believe in these blessings and that through our faith and the will of the Lord, miracles can happen. This is what I've always been taught from a young age.

In the Bible, James 5:14–15(KJV) it says:

14. Is any sick among you? Let him call for the elders of the church; and let them pray over him, anointing him with oil in the name of the Lord:

15. And the prayer of faith shall save the sick, and the Lord shall raise him up; and if he have committed sins, they shall be forgiven him.

I will never forget the words my dad said as I closed my eyes and hoped for the best outcome of the terrible situation

29

we were in. His words are ones that I have thought over and over again throughout the last ten years.

> *"Jason Frederick Behle. By the power of the Melchizedek priesthood in which we hold, the same power Jesus used to raise the dead, I command you to rise...if it be God's will. In the name of Jesus Christ, amen."*

Never before had I felt or been a part of a prayer or blessing more powerful than this.

The word faith can be described as having *"Complete trust or confidence in someone or something."*

I had faith in what my dad said. I had faith in the power we held and in our personal relationships with God. I knew my dad was guided to say what he did. He asked for him to rise, but we also knew that it wasn't our final decision to make. We put our trust in God. My dad had complete faith in the Lord and asked him to do his will. He didn't ask for what he wanted, of course he wanted his son to wake from that hospital bed and be fine, instead he asked that God do his will, whatever that may be.

By this time my mom had arrived. We all stepped outside the room and they closed the curtain to continue working on him. These were his friends and co-workers. They were the ones that picked him up in the ambulance earlier at his house. In fact, my brother received a call on his work radio asking if he was available to help. His friend

Mike said over the radio that it was a young male who had stopped breathing and they could use his assistance on the call. Jason's wife picked up the radio and declared, "He can't help you; it's Jason that needs the help. The emergency call is for him. He needs your help. Mike, please get here fast."

Earlier that night, he went on an emergency call involving a young lady that had overdosed on drugs. They were able to revive her, and he was thrilled as he explained this to Michelle when he got home around 2 a.m. This girl had another shot at living, and they played a huge part in this. It made him proud she had another chance.

After they fell asleep, his wife later woke to head to work for a couple hours. She had a babysitter come over to watch their five-year-old daughter and two-year-old son while he slept after being out so late on a call. She returned home a little later to find he was still in bed in their room.

She knew he needed to help us with the sprinklers so she went in to wake him and to get his butt over to help us out. As she entered the room, she found him lying there, only he wasn't breathing.

When they first met, they were both working at the University of Utah Hospital. Little did she know that the training she received there would someday be used to give her own husband CPR. She called for help, knowing that the medics to arrive would be his friends and co-workers on the ambulance he had just finished a shift on hours earlier. I will always admire her for doing what she did. I couldn't imagine what she went through finding her spouse unconscious and having to administer him CPR.

Back at the hospital after we had given him a blessing, we stood outside his room waiting for what seemed forever. After a while my mom noticed the feet of those working on him under the curtain and that they stopped moving as fast as they had initially been. Just then, the doctor opened the curtain and stepped out of the room. The look on his face is one I'll never forget.

"I am sorry. He's gone. We couldn't bring him back. We did everything we could."

I'm sure it never gets easier for a doctor when they tell family and loved ones news like this. We pretty much knew the outcome already, and we knew that if they had been able to revive him, he had gone so long without oxygen to the brain that he would have probably been brain dead, but still, hearing the doctor say this finalized the worst outcome. Being present while someone tells the parents that their child died is something I never hope to experience again.

I remember a lot about that day... mainly that everything became a huge blur.

I yelled "NO" as I ran out the hallway and slipped as I turned the corner. From the top of my lungs, I blurted out some choice words that probably shouldn't have been yelled in public let alone at a quiet small town hospital. I must have looked like a mad man running outside screaming.

I had just received the hardest news up to this point of my life and watched a doctor tell my parents what no parent should ever have to hear. If I looked like a crazy person; I was okay with that, because in reality at that time, I was one.

I darted outside to the front of the hospital and found some lawn to crash on. I couldn't think, I couldn't move. I was motionless, but knew I needed to find strength in order to call my sister Keri and my brothers Mike and Ty. My parents asked me to tell them the news of their oldest brother. They were easily the three most difficult and horrible phone calls I've ever had to make.

I remembered back to several years before this, I was home with my mom when she received a call about my sister's best friend being killed in a car crash. I went into the room with my mom as she told her what she had just learned over the phone. As she began to tell Keri, I literally had to grab my sister and stop her from falling straight to the ground in shock.

I held on and squeezed as my sister sobbed. Death brings out the rawest form of emotions for people as we realize how vulnerable we all are. Life really is so short.

My sister has been through her share of dealing with death at such a young age. About three years ago, several years after Jason had died, I got a call from Keri, who was living in Idaho with her husband Jordan and their kids. She was crying. She told me that Jordan's little brother was just killed in a car accident. Hearing this kind of news never gets easier. Life is fragile.

As I told my siblings the news, each of them reacted in their own way of being shocked. Keri instantly started weeping over the phone. Mike had just got out of the shower. Out of anger, hurt and frustration he punched a hole in his closet door after we hung up. Tyler was driving in the neighborhood, headed home, and his friend in the the passenger seat had to grab the wheel to steer as he dropped his hands in disbelief and pretty much stopped functioning.

I called my then girlfriend, now beautiful wife Jena, and told her as well. She was and is still such a huge strength to me. She dropped everything and drove out to the hospital with Keri. Mike, his then girlfriend and now wife Kelly drove out together with Tyler. We hung around the hospital for a little while waiting for other family members to arrive before the mortuary needed to take his lifeless body away.

The face of my grandfather Papa, who was seventy-seven at the time, is one that will always stick with me. He walked into the hospital crying and pleading with the lord to take him instead of his grandson.

"He is so young, I am old. I have lived a good long life. Take me instead," he pleaded.

The dreaded thought of needing to tell his kids the news weighed heavy on all of us. I mean, how do you tell a five and two-year-old that their dad died? Later that night after returning home from the hospital. The kid's mom, Michelle sat them down individually and explained to them that their daddy went to heaven to live with Jesus. Mykell, the five-year-old, looked right up at her with a comforting smile and said

"I know, mommy, Jesus told me."

"Blessed are the pure in heart: for they shall see God."
—Matthew 5:8 (KJV)

Kids really do have the purest hearts.

One of the hardest moments personally, was when my dad later approached me with tears in his eyes and apologizing that he didn't have enough faith to bring Jason back. I could literally feel his pain and knew it was deeper than I could possibly comprehend, not being a father myself at the time.

Here was a man that gave everything he could to the Lord and his family. I saw a hurt that I hope to never see in anyone again. My parents were now going to be burying their oldest child. No parent should ever have to go through this.

It was extremely hard to hear my father apologize. I knew that if anyone could have brought my brother back aside from Jesus himself, it would have been my dad. I knew he had faith to do so, but to hear him doubt and blame himself after the fact was difficult and showed how humble my father truly is.

All we had to go on was that God had a different plan that day. He was in control of things. His will be done. Don't we pray for this?

Years later, I would learn what a struggle it can be to accept this simple truth.

5

*"Go into the world and do well. But more
importantly, go into the world and do good."*
—Minor Myers

"Where is Ty, has anyone seen him?"

"He was right here just a minute ago," someone
said, looking around for him.

"I'll go look outside to see if he went for some fresh
air." I told my family.

They had just taken Jason's body away to the mortuary
and we were getting ready to head back home, only we
couldn't find Ty. He's the youngest of the family and at the
time was nearly eighteen years old.

I called his phone. "Where are you, bro?"

"I'm at Jason's house, he said, with cracking in his voice
and full of pain.

After he said his goodbyes to Jason before they took
him, he walked a couple blocks over to his house.

"What are you doing there?" I asked. "We're getting
ready to leave and no one could find you."

He said "I have to finish it. I promised I'd help him finish the dog run. It's not done yet and now he's gone."

Like all of us, he was hurting.

The day before he had been out there helping put in the dog run for Tahoe, the big black lab. They hadn't quite finished it as the concrete post needed to dry overnight, so Ty decided to head over and finish what they had started just the day before.

I grabbed my dad's Jeep to go pick him up. Even in Ty's pain, he wanted to serve. This was something our parents taught us and we watched our older brother do so many times before.

In high school, I didn't want to follow Jason's careless ways, but it was now years later and I wanted to be more like him. He served others for no reason other than that it was simply the right thing to do. He was constantly helping someone out. His medical career was one of service and when he wasn't on shift he was helping a neighbor with something else. His sprinkler installation business was never really profitable because he hardly charged anyone for his work. He just liked to offer a hand to anyone in need. I remember clearly getting a call from him years ago.

"Hey bro, what are you doing this Saturday?"

"Not sure," I said, "don't really have any plans yet."

"Perfect, because I already scheduled some stuff for us to do. I'll call Mike and Ty and the three of you can come out together and meet me at my house Saturday morning."

The war in Iraq had just started and he thought it would be cool to find some homes where the husbands had been deployed and go over and do yard work for their families.

The four of us spent the Saturday at three or four different houses doing whatever work they needed done around the yard. We took our mowers, trimmers, rakes and shovels. What a good day working and serving with my brothers. We felt good knowing we were doing something for the heroes that were out serving the country and giving back, even in such a small way.

After a day's hard work, we went over to Jason's for one of his famous juicy barbecue hamburgers accompanied with his secret recipe, baked beans, that I swear will clog an artery if you eat too much at one time.

To this day, this is one of my favorite memories and something I think back on often. Serving with my brothers and hanging out afterwards, eating, what a great way to spend a Saturday.

We had nothing to gain by setting up this service project and I am glad he decided to do it anyway. It was nice showing these families we cared and appreciated what their husband and fathers were doing for all of us. The families were sacrificing a lot while their loved one was away, kind of making our pulling weeds and mowing lawns seem trivial, yet it left a lasting impression on me all these years later.

At my brother's funeral, it was great to hear from so many people on whom he had left a positive impact. When my time is up, I hope to leave a lasting mark like he has. I hope that my funeral is packed with people that I have influenced for the better. It truly felt as though the theme of his funeral was service. Story after story kept pouring in from people he had helped.

Was my brother perfect? Of course, he wasn't. We often immortalize those that have passed with only the best stories and memories of them. I've already mentioned many of his faults; I think the key is to strive to leave more positive than negative marks. I'm convinced my brother did this.

He left the faith we were raised in nearly ten years before he died, but in the last year of his life he had made some steps towards a personal relationship with his maker. We knew he was on a good path and I often wonder if he maybe subconsciously knew he would meet God sooner than later and perhaps this helped him to get on the path he was on.

I learned wonderful lessons from him about serving and caring for others. I also found the joy in doing so and loved how it made a person feel. Going through this and seeing all the help we received from so many friends and strangers gave me a different perspective.

My parents have always called me their compassionate child and said I'm really tender-hearted. In high school, I always tried to be the opposite of this because I was afraid of looking weak. My senior year I buzzed my head, grew a long goatee and hit people as hard as I could on the football field. Even though my love was playing baseball, I put the effort into football because most of my buddies were on the team and we had great camaraderie. Our coach was also an inspiring guy that I knew I could learn a lot from.

We liked the idea of thinking we ruled the school. We rumbled with anyone or any group that tried to challenge us.

Looking back, I realize it's so important to be true to yourself and to not do things to look cool to your peers. I feel bad about some of the ways I treated others. I often walked around with a chip on my shoulder, ready to take on the world, if needed. I knew that wasn't me. We had a lot of fun in those days, but I wish I had been a little more kind to those around me who were not directly inside my circle of friends.

The truth is, even to this day I like to try and keep somewhat of a tough guy image. Even though I try my best to treat others right, I like to always keep an edge. I think that's one of the reasons I bought my Harley in the first place. Tough guys ride Harleys. When was the last time you saw a sissy riding one? Especially with long ape hanger handlebars and a suicide stick shift like I have on mine. The biker image has always intrigued me.

I remember while attending college, I would often daydream during lectures. I was doing my general studies the school makes you get through before taking advanced classes on subjects you are interested in.

I'd sit in class mostly bored out of my mind and entertain the thought of loading up some gear, strapping it to my bike and taking off with no plan other than seeing the country. Freedom on the road seemed like the perfect life. No more working just to pay my way through college for classes I didn't want to take. The open road was what I longed for.

Of course, I'd wake from this daydream and realize that probably wasn't the most responsible thing to do. I ignored the urge, which now I look back on and, knowing how short life really is, I wish I had actually taken such a cool motorcycle road trip. After all, we're never promised a tomorrow.

6

*"I've seen and met angels wearing the disguise
of ordinary people living ordinary lives."*
—Tracy Chapman

Time heals. I've heard this often. I've experienced it,
yet here we are ten years down the road and I'm still
dealing with grief. Is this normal? I don't know; I do know
that there hasn't been a day in ten years that I haven't had at
least one thought about my brother Jason.

At first, they were sad thoughts. I guess time does heal,
because as the years have passed by, the sad ones have turned
into more happy ones. My parents and family have done
a great job at keeping his memory and legacy alive. Every
Memorial Day and on his death day, we meet at his grave
and tell stories. It's a great way for us to remember him and
for all our little ones to hear about the uncle that had passed
before they were born.

My family has had some experiences that we consider
subtle reminders from my brother telling us that we're closer
than we realize. In little ways he lets us know he is watching

over us. These have been strength builders and have helped ease the sting of death.

We've heard before that there are angels amongst us. I believe this to be true; in fact, I consider that I live with one every day: my beautiful Jena.

She has been my saving grace throughout our married life. She's been my rock from day one. After our first date, I told my sister I was going to marry her. I used to make fun of my friends that would say the same thing after going out for such a short time with a girl, but here I was telling my sister the same thing. I think she thought it was a joke and part of me did as well, but for some reason, I knew it would happen and boy am I glad that it did.

We only dated for eight months when I bought a ring to propose to her. Even though it was a short courtship that started when we met at Utah Valley University in Orem, Utah, from our very first date, I don't think we ever spent a day apart afterwards. I knew there was something special about her and I wanted to seal the deal.

I planned to propose after dinner in downtown Salt Lake City and had set up a carriage ride to a historical mansion that had beautiful gardens and a large castle-like staircase out front. I wanted to walk her up the stairs, grab her hand and get down on one knee. After she hopefully said yes, Jason was going to be hiding behind the mansion and let off some aerial fireworks, making it the perfect princess proposal I thought she deserved.

Sometimes life has a different plan than that of its own. This case was no different. Instead of getting engaged that Saturday evening, we spent the day laying my brother to rest.

About a week after he died, I remember my grandmother Mum pulling me aside and asking what my plan with Jena was. When was I going to propose to her? I said I didn't feel right about the timing. We were all in the middle of mourning and I thought it would be selfish of me to turn the attention to my own engagement.

Mum told me the complete opposite of what I was thinking.

"Brad, the family needs something positive to look ahead to," she said. "You should ask her to marry you soon."

I think she and everyone else feared that if I dragged my feet any longer, I'd lose my shot with Jena and we all knew how far out of my league she is, so I couldn't let this happen. My grandmother thought if I let her go, I would never find anyone close to her caliber to replace her, which was true.

A week later, I surprised Jena with Tim McGraw tickets at an outdoor concert venue for her birthday. It would be the perfect time and place for me to propose to her. I knew there would be radio stations giving away prizes and playing games, so I talked with them beforehand and had a plan all set up.

We stood in line to spin a giant wheel trying to win what they were giving away. It was her turn to spin. She stepped up and gave it a whirl. I was nervous and wanted it to keep spinning and spinning, but then it stopped. The DJ looked over at us and started loudly announcing over his live microphone:

"We have a winner! Congratulations. You just won the grand prize." She was excited and started jumping up and down wondering what the grand prize could possibly be? She turned over to the crowd of people that were clapping and then glanced back over at me. By this time, I was down on one knee holding the ring in my hand.

Only two weeks had passed since Jason died and more than ever after she had been such strength to me these past weeks, I wanted to be with her for the rest of my life.

I asked her to make me the happiest man ever and she said yes. The crowd that witnessed it started clapping and yelling congratulations. It was really fun and made the concert that night even more special.

This wasn't how I had originally planned to propose, it wasn't the cute fairytale story I wanted to give her, but it was perfect for the time. It was a complete surprise to her as she thought I would hold off for a while to let things settle down.

We planned a quick engagement and two months later we had a beautiful marriage ceremony. It was a short time to plan it all, but we were ready to get on with it and start our lives together. We planned two receptions, one night in Mapleton, Utah for her family and friends and one in Salt Lake City for mine.

They both were beautiful. It was almost the middle of September, and it can be risky to plan outdoor receptions with Utah weather, but both days turned out great and the weather couldn't have been better either of the nights.

The second reception was on top of my dad's building, the same one just two months earlier we were working at and waiting for my brother to show up to help. It was a good experience holding the reception there, even though the memories of that day were still so fresh.

After the reception ended, we took the elevator down and walked out the door to find around thirty of my friends' motorcycles lining State Street to escort us away. My Harley had cans tied to the back and a sign that read "Just married".

Jena, still in her beautiful white wedding dress and me in my black tux with biker boots loaded up on my Harley, we all fired up the hogs and let them roar. My friend 'Big Dave' shot some flames out his exhaust and then we took off. Uncle Scott led the way as we rode down the street getting waves from all the passing cars. The next morning we left for our honeymoon in Cancun, a week of the ocean, sun and just being together.

7

"Tender mercies of the Lord are real and that they do not occur randomly or merely by coincidence." —*David Bednar*

We all experience loss in this life. It's part of living; all of us will die. There is no escaping it. Knowing this, does it make it easier when dealing with losing someone you love? I don't know. I do know what made it easier for me and my family was all of the loving support from so many.

People came out of the woodwork to help us with whatever they could think of or anything we needed. It was inspiring and strengthened my faith in humanity and my perspective of the good in the world. Regardless of what you see on the news and the bad going on everywhere, if you look closely, you'll see there is so much good around us all. I am forever grateful to those that helped me see this by serving our family at this difficult time.

As the one-year mark of his death date was approaching, we wanted to do something to give back and show appreciation for the love we were shown. My brother loved kids, his two were everything to him. I knew if we were to raise some money for a charity, we should find a local one that serves children.

Knowing my brother loved to ride motorcycles and still feeling guilty for not letting him borrow my bike for the firefighter/paramedic charity ride years before, I thought it would be cool to organize a little biker rally of our own and to end it with a barbecue like he would have wanted. I approached my family and they were all in favor of it and thought it was a great idea.

I called around to some local organizations and asked about their mission and where the donated money would go. After trying several different ones, I didn't feel like I had found the right charity that fit the criteria we were looking for.

I asked my mom her thoughts and she remembered her good friend's husband Stewart was running a children's charity in Salt Lake. It was considered an umbrella charity that raised money through their large events and then would disperse it to several smaller local children's benefit organizations that they felt were doing good things.

I loved this idea; they focused on kids and were helping in a lot of different ways. Their reach was wide on who they could help.

I contacted Stewart and explained to him our idea and plan for the event. He invited me to visit him at his office the following week so we could sit down and discuss how to get the ball rolling.

The following week I found myself sitting around a conference table with him and another executive of the foundation they worked for. As we discussed the future event, we talked about ideas for marketing and publicity. I wanted to spread the word about this charity ride, but also wanted to keep it small enough to be manageable, since it was our first year doing this.

They both liked the idea for a benefit and then showed me where the money would go within their organization if we donated it to them. I felt like that was important to see how they would be spending it. After seeing the programs, it would help support, I was excited for us to help further their cause.

I was only twenty-five at the time and felt pretty official sitting in the boardroom around a table with these two successful men, bouncing ideas off each other on how to make the event really work.

I had met Stewart a couple times before through my mom and knew that he had lost his son ten or eleven years ago, and learned this was one of the reasons he was working with a children's organization. Even though years had gone by since his son passed, as we sat in his office, he told me the story and I could sense his pain. I appreciated him sharing his feelings with me.

As the event got closer, my whole family was in charge of lining up donations for the auction with different companies they had connections to. We ended up getting quite a lot of items donated which was another way I saw the good in people and their willingness to help.

My mom was a superstar in helping to plan this ride. She is so much more organized than I am. Planning and organizing this event was good for all of us and I think it helped my parents with the ongoing pain of losing their oldest child just a year earlier.

It's amazing what can happen when you do things and serve others; it's really a powerful way to heal. I think as a family, we all were feeling this as it gave us a positive purpose to pursue. There are so many people that have it a lot worse than we do, so it felt nice to help and give to others in need.

This first year we kept the ride and barbecue pretty intimate with family members and friends. As I mentioned before, to me all bikers were thought of as friends and any that wanted to ride for a good cause were welcome to join. This was before the Facebook days of creating an event and inviting your friends online. I actually had to go around and hand out flyers to hang on the walls of some of my favorite bike shops. I also let my biker buddies know about the ride and the cause we were raising money for.

After Jason died, I thought about the word *paradise* often. I named my landscape company Paradise Scapes and also sold hammocks I imported from Paraguay, calling them Abit'A Paradise. My sales pitch was telling people we all needed down time and what better way than swinging in a hammock and relaxing?

Is Paradise where my brother went after passing through this life? What does this word mean to other people? Is it the sandy beach with the crashing ocean waves and palm trees or the mountains with a cool breeze rustling the aspen leaves and smell of pinecones from the surrounding trees? I often ask people what their idea of this perfect place is for them?

As I mentioned earlier, to me the dictionary defines it best. It's a state of bliss.

After a lot of thought, I decided on calling the event the **R**ide **I**n **P**aradise (**RIP**). I often wondered and studied about where my brother possibly was. The name felt right for this charity ride. It would represent where he was and how it's a peaceful state of mind. The RIP gave the tough biker image where I could incorporate skulls and make it look cool in the logo, cause remember, I need things to look tough.

Just this year, I had Ty take a picture of me riding my Harley down the street. When he sent it over to me, I couldn't believe how much it looked like the logo I had made up nearly ten years before for this ride. The one he took is the one I decided to use for the cover of this book.

The day we picked for the charity ride and event was July 2, 2005, the Saturday before his one-year death date. My uncle Scott and I decided all the riders would meet up around Immigration Canyon at 5 pm. We would ride up, go around East Canyon reservoir and then head back down. It was a beautiful ride to go on and one we have done many times before. We thought it would be a great route to take and all the riders would enjoy getting up in the mountains and through the canyon where the temperature was a little cooler and they could ride through the beautiful scenery.

Jena and I went over to Sugar House Park to help get the pavilion ready that we rented for the after-ride barbecue. We then went to meet the other riders while those that weren't riding stayed back to finish up for when everyone arrived.

Jena rode on the back of my bike and we met with my uncle Scott and aunt Carlene who was riding on the back of his Fatboy. We arrived at the parking lot at the base of the canyon to wait for the others.

I was nervous. I had never planned an event like this before and didn't know what to expect or how many people and bikes would show up.

It was just after 5 pm as we waited for any stragglers to show up before we decided to take off and hit the road up the canyon. There were around thirty bikes with several others riding double up. We thought it was a pretty good turnout for the inaugural event.

I was even more nervous now, especially because I was the lead bike and everyone would be following my speed and route.

I gathered everyone together and started thanking them for coming. I reminded them of the cause of honoring my brother who had served so many people in his short years and to anyone else that had a loved one that had passed on they wanted to ride for. We were also raising some money for a great children's charity organization.

As I was speaking to the group, I was holding my phone in my hand so I could check the time to know when to start the ride and answer it in case anyone was lost and needed directions to get there.

Just then my phone vibrated in my hand. I was mid-sentence as I looked down to see who was calling. My eyes immediately filled with tears as I choked up and briefly couldn't speak.

"How could this be?" I thought.

I couldn't believe what was flashing across the screen of my phone.

"Jason calling"

I watched it ring a couple times but was nervous about actually answering it. I felt a peaceful sensation come over me.

I went to press the answer button but was too late. The screen now read:

"Missed call from Jason"

I stood silently for a moment as I thought of a memory from his funeral a year before. The mortuary had done a nice job preparing his body so we could see it before saying our final goodbyes. We each took a couple minutes with him. I thought back to my time as I took off my guardian angel motorcycle pin I was wearing and placed it on his suit jacket lapel. As I did this, I hoped that he would help protect me as I rode my bike and thought that maybe he would ride with me sometimes.

After we all had our moment of goodbyes, we offered a family prayer before closing the casket and escorting it into the chapel for the service to begin.

I subtly wiped my tears as I reminisced back on this experience, but knew I needed to put on my tough face and finish explaining the route. "Saddle up, let's ride!"

I hurried and called the number back knowing that my grandparents had taken over his phone after he passed. It was my Grandmother Mum, she was wondering when we were leaving so they could gauge on when to start cooking the burgers and to have things ready for our arrival.

To this day, ten years later, that number is still saved in my contact list under my brother's name. It's always a cool reminder whenever I get a call from them to have a quick thought of my bro.

At the time, a mobile phone was still new to them and they mainly had it for emergency situations only. In the last year since they got the phone, I had never received a call from them from that number. They always used their home line.

This call was too coincidental for me to not think that for one little moment my brother was calling from beyond. Those that have passed on are closer than we probably realize. I was grateful to feel this, and I knew he was proud of what we were doing. He would be watching over us as we rode and possibly be like the guardian angel, I put on his jacket the year before.

8

"In three words I can sum up everything I've learned about life: it goes on."—Robert Frost

Life was good. I loved being married to my sweetheart and was amazed every day at what was becoming of my life. As much as you miss those that have passed on and even though you feel them close at times, life continues on and it can be great.

Our first apartment had two small bedrooms and was one that we knew we would someday look back on and laugh that we called this place our home. It was in Sandy, Utah. The owner converted an old house to a loan office complex on the middle floor. The basement was a one-bedroom apartment and ours was a two bedroom on the top floor. They each had separate entrances, so we had some privacy, even though there were people coming in and out the whole day looking for a loan. We stayed there eight or nine months.

At the time Jena was working as a health unit coordinator for a local hospital. She started there right out of high school and had always wanted to become a nurse. I was working for my uncle's property maintenance company and didn't really have any desire to go back to school.

The week before Jason passed, he was let go from his job. He had his family and a new house with a mortgage. It was a tough time. I knew this extra stress added to his sudden death. When he passed, we were told it was sleep apnea and tonsillitis. He pretty much just stopped breathing in his sleep.

I used the excuse of him being laid off from Corporate America as a reason to not go back to school, but really it was out of bitterness and not having a good reason why I should. I didn't really enjoy school. I had just finished my General Education requirements, enough for my associates of science degree, and since I didn't really know what I wanted to specialize in, I didn't care to go back.

I'm glad I went the two and a half years I did go and was able to meet Jena while at school, but knew I eventually would want to start my own business instead. I later found this to be easier said than done and at times a secure paycheck from an employer every two weeks has sounded really nice. Don't get me wrong, I'm a creative and driven person who enjoys doing his own thing, but sometimes the logistics of running a business can be harder than one thinks and as a business owner you end up wearing all the hats of your small company.

Jena had just learned she was accepted into the nursing program through her work, which was a huge blessing. There was no waiting list and they paid for the whole two-year program. She just needed to commit to working for them for a couple years after graduation. She had already been there nearly five years, so we figured this wouldn't be a problem, especially since the majority of the hospitals in Utah are run by the same company. She could transfer to any one of them if we ever moved or if she wanted a change.

I decided to branch out on my own and started a landscaping business from the ground up. I also started selling hammocks that I imported from Paraguay and Mexico on the side. I sold them at trade shows and started an e-commerce site. It was early 2005 and online shopping was still new territory for a lot of people, so it didn't do very well in e-commerce. I mostly sold them at the shows and to my landscaping clients for their backyards.

Things were going well; we were busy and happy. My sweet wife worked full time putting herself through nursing school. It was pretty intense for her and I realized even more how lucky I was to find this loving woman. She aced all of her exams and finished the program at the top of her class.

I had been building up my landscaping business and I didn't take a paycheck for a year and a half so I could pay off my equipment as I got the business up and running.

In the winter months when the lawns I maintained were covered in snow, I worked as a sales associate for a fitness equipment company. I enjoyed this and the commission money was typically pretty good as people were buying during these months for Christmas and New Year's resolutions.

We didn't have a lot of bills and lived simply so were able to take time to travel. We loved anywhere warm. We went on a couple of cruises to the Bahamas, and we took a trip to Maui to celebrate Jena's nursing school graduation, along with several visits to Lake Powell and other fun places.

It was on this Maui trip that I came to the realization I wanted to try something new for work. I had landscaped pretty much my whole life up to this point and was really enjoying the fitness business I was working in. Staying fit was a large part of my life growing up in athletics, and when I worked in the industry during the winter months, I enjoyed it. Only I wanted not to sell the equipment, but rather be the one to help people use it to get in shape.

I was in a car accident a year earlier and had really hurt my back. I had two bulging discs in my lower spine and tried everything short of surgery to lessen the pain and discomfort. I always kept myself in great shape but learned that my all-around core was weak. I had focused on "mirror muscles" mainly and after doing some research decided to start doing some functional training and seeing if I could help my back by strengthening my core muscles.

After seeing such good results from this, I wanted to help train and teach other people with these methods.

Kettlebells had been a huge tool in strengthening my back and core so I decided to go to Vegas and become certified as an instructor in the summer of 2008. I came home and opened a fitness training franchise business that specializes in early morning boot camps.

Jena was now working as a nurse in the medical telemetry unit where they dealt a lot with cardiac patients. She's a wonderful nurse but was working long hours and crazy graveyard shifts. I again was starting a new business from the ground up after selling my landscaping one.

To add to the chaos, we decided we wanted to start having kids. We had been living in the townhome we bought three years before but now wanted to find a house out by Utah Lake. I just restored an old ski boat and we were driving out thirty minutes there and back a couple times a week to wakeboard, so we decided to start looking at some homes in the growing area. It's a little far out there, some would say, but there were great deals and at the time you could get more home for your money. It was the spring of 2009 and there was a large inventory of homes since the crash of 2008 had happened just months before and still was affecting the market. It was a scary time to buy, not knowing if the economy would get worse, I had a new startup business and Jena was pregnant with our son, Bode. We found a too good to pass up deal on a brand-new home that the bank took from the builder after he went under. We decided to pull the trigger on it and see if we could get it.

We had looked at several homes and didn't really see anything we wanted to act on. Then we walked into this one.

"This is our home; this is perfect for our new little family," Jena said.

The realtor and I both had doubts. It was a little more money than we wanted to spend, even though it was a great value, with the bank wanting to unload it. We put in an offer and about a week later heard back from the bank. They said they had decided to go with a higher bid.

"It's our house, you just wait and see" Jena said after I told her the news. Two hours later, the bank called me back. They felt more comfortable with our offer and credit history. She was right about the house. It was ours!

With things going as they were. I felt blessed. We kept to our faith and attended church every week. It had now been five years since my brother passed. I accepted this reality and with time it became easier to deal with. I missed seeing him, but also knew people had it much worse than we did and he was in a good place. I was feeling really fortunate for how my life was turning out.

My brother's wife had since remarried and moved up to Idaho. We didn't see his kids as often as we'd like to with them far away, but we were all starting to have our own kids and giving my parents new grandchildren to spoil. Even though they missed Jason's kids like crazy, having more grandkids around seemed to help them with the pain.

As it got closer to us becoming first-time parents, my perception started to shift. I started thinking a little differently about the loss of my brother.

When our son Bode was born, I couldn't believe the love I felt. I thought I had experienced love before but was blown away at this whole new level and depth I was experiencing by having a child of my own.

A perfect little boy that got me excited for the days ahead playing ball out in the yard, going to his games and wrestling each other on the ground. What would he turn out to be like? I wondered. Everything is so new to him and the world is wide open, full of great things for him to experience.

As he grew and I lived the joy of having a newborn child (apart from the sleepless night, thousands of dirty diapers and schedule changes), I couldn't help but think of the pain my parents must have felt as they buried their oldest child just five years earlier. At one time, years earlier, my father held his firstborn just as I was now. Excited for his future and for all the things he would experience and accomplish.

My mindset changed. Yes, I lost my older brother, but how could I ever deal with losing my son? How can anybody? I thought of my parents and others that have lost a child. I realized how strong they must be and was encouraged by their strength to get through hard things that seemed so unimaginable as this.

My parents are great examples to us as a family and the glue that holds us all together.

Jason 9, Brad 7 jumping down a sandhill. 1986

Riding my grandparents Honda Passport in
St. George, Utah with my dad. 1987

Leaving our wedding with 30 motorcycles, September
2004. Uncle Scott laughing and leading the way.

Jason fishing with his son Luke. 3 days
before he passed. July 2004

Jena, Luke and I after the 1st 'Ride In
Paradise' charity ride. July 2005

The article I found in my desk the night I couldn't sleep.

Delivering a giant teddy bear with my son, Bode. 2014

Delivering a teddy bear and book with my niece, Mykell.

Doing a 'Ride In Paradise' with Keaton's
parents, Scott and Kimberli

To whomever rode their Harley Davidson up our
driveway, dropped this off, knocked on the door and
drove off...THANK YOU♥. Personally, I needed this
tonight. Somewhat of a rough day. Thank you is not
sufficient for the love you delivered this evening! 🧸
🐻

The reason for these rides. Seeing messages like this.

Love for two wheels passed down from my
parents. Date night on their scooters. 2016

Last Behle family trip before 'Papa' passed. July 2020

My kids snuggling their 'Papa bears' from
the Springer family after dad passed.

Jason Behle June 23, 1977 - July 6, 2004

Keaton Howard August 20, 2007 - June 28, 2013

Fred Behle July 15, 1952 - February 25, 2021

9

"Be kind to everyone you meet, for we are all facing a hard battle." —Unknown source

Bode had just turned two in July and it was now mid-October. Jena abruptly woke me up at 3:30 am.

"Brad, my water just broke."

No, it didn't, you probably just wet the bed." I thought I was so funny and proud to be so witty after waking up so suddenly in the middle of the night.

"Brad, I'm serious. We need to go!" she blurts out, showing she was not kidding around. Our baby girl was coming!

I hopped out of bed and grabbed our bags and helped her to the car as we called our Moms. Jena had invited them and our grandmothers to be in the room to experience the birth of our daughter Solee, so we needed to let them know what was going on and we were headed to the hospital.

We left the house and the contractions were getting closer, so I put the gas pedal closer to the floor and a couple minutes later, I got pulled over. I was doing 95 mph in a 55 mph zone. I believe that's terms for impounding a car...

"Is there a reason you're speeding?" The officer asked.

"Yes, my wife is pregnant and the baby is coming...like coming right now!"

She poked her head into our car and asked her if this was true? Before Jena could even answer, the officer could see it in her eyes and told us to slow down, be careful, but to get to the hospital, quickly.

We arrived around 5 a.m. Our precious daughter made her entrance at 5:51. That was a close one! What an experience it was. Neither our Moms nor grandmothers had witnessed a birth apart from the birth of their own kids, so it was really cool to have them there for this and witness one of life's biggest miracles, the birth of a child.

I now had two beautiful, healthy little kids. A great house, careers we both enjoyed and some savings in the bank. Sharing this all with the woman I love, life was really good. On the outside. The truth was I was dealing with some major inner turmoil. Why was I feeling so torn up inside? Why did I feel bitter and filled with doubt? I questioned things I once thought were so true, I could never doubt them. Yet, here I was.

Looking back now, I think I held some things deep down inside of me. I don't think I ever really took time to let myself experience grief and truly work through it. My parents went to support groups, but I never felt like I needed to. I was good. Life became so busy quickly after my brother's death with our marriage, Jena's school, and starting a couple different businesses that I don't think I ever took the time to work through some issues I had that were just now surfacing. When I started having my own kids and feeling a different kind of love that comes with being a parent. I started aching for my parents and for their immense loss.

Not long after he died, while going through some of his stuff we found a letter he had written to a doctor asking for help. We were aware of some of his personal struggles, but seeing this letter brought more light to it, only it was now too late to do anything to help him.

My dad introduced us at a young age to skiing, one of his passions. We loved to snow ski together. As we got older and Jason had graduated high school, He became a ski bum and went almost every day during the winter months. He was pretty good and liked to brag about the jumps and backflips he'd do off the kickers at the resorts. He could also fly down the mountain with great form and could ski the moguls beautifully.

One winter day we were up at Alta Ski Resort and the conditions were perfect, great snow and a bluebird sky. It was our last run and we were directly below the lift where you had to ski your best because everyone riding it was watching from above.

There was this big old jump and he decided to backflip off it at the last second. as he landed, we both heard a loud pop! He fell to the ground in pain. After a couple minutes he got up and tried to make his way down the mountain. He couldn't put much pressure on his leg and would immediately fall as he tried to turn. It was the lateral movement that hurt the worst, which made us fear he probably tore a major ligament in his knee.

I ended up skiing down quickly and finding Ski Patrol to come and help him down the rest of the mountain. They put him on the sled and dragged him to the lodge.

We went home, told our parents what had happened, and mom made a doctor appointment. A couple days later my parents sat in the room with him waiting for the doctor to bring in his knee X-rays. The news he brought was far worse than what they had expected. Not only had he torn his ligament, but there was a substantially large tumor on his knee. He would need surgery soon to have it removed, the doctor strongly recommended.

That night at home my dad gave Jason a blessing. He directly blessed that the doctor would check his knee again before the surgery and that the tumor would be gone. A couple days later, as the doctor looked over some new X-rays preparing for the surgery, the tumor was nowhere to be found. The doctor was shocked and had never seen such a large and noticeable tumor disappear like this one. As a family we knew what had happened and were grateful for the power of prayer.

Even with this great news he wasn't out of the woods just yet. He still needed surgery to repair his ACL.

The surgery went as well as can be expected and he was on the road to recovery; unfortunately, it can be a painful one. He was prescribed Lortab to help with the pain management and discomfort.

Sure, he messed around a little bit in high school. I told you about the weed falling into his truck vent and I also witnessed some crazy drinking experiences with him and his friends, but this was different. Like many others that fall into this trap of prescription drugs, he wasn't out searching for a high, not at first. He was looking for relief post-surgery by using what was doctor prescribed.

Little did any of us know the demon that was awakened and how hard of a battle it would be.

For years as a family, we were aware of this struggle. We tried to help any way we could. Addiction is a damn awful thing. It is a beast buried inside that is always persistently working to take over your life.

It's something that has become so common in our society today, but it's still taboo to talk about. There are many forms of addictions many of us struggle with, yet in our quest for perfection and looking good to others, it's not typically something we like to discuss and something that many look down on. Those battling can feel hopeless. Society thinks it just better to sweep it under the rug and pass the victims off as druggies, creeps or losers.

One of the most difficult things for me to handle was the letter we found months after he died that he had recently written to a doctor. It shows his emotional pain and fear. He was nearing rock bottom and was scared he would lose the things that are the most important to him. I admire his strength to reach out. Many times, we are too afraid to ask for help when it's really needed. Even though the outcome wasn't what we wanted, it shows he was able to humble himself and recognize that he couldn't get better on his own.

There was a newer prescription drug out he learned about. People were having success with it kicking their habits with other narcotics. I don't really understand the mentality of fighting a drug addiction with another potentially addictive one, but doctors were raving about this and rehabilitation centers were using it on their patients.

My brother was desperate for help. You can see the severity of it here in the letter we found.

TO WHOM IT MAY CONCERN:

My name is Jason Behle. I have had an addiction to pain medication for about 5 years now. It started off with a knee surgery that I had. I had a hard time discontinuing that I was prescribed. The medication that I first had a problem with was lortab. After taking the lortab for a while, I was able to get prescriptions for ultram. The doctor said that it would help with the pain and I wouldn't get addicted to it. I soon was addicted. I would go between lortab and ultram for several years until I just would use lortab or whatever prescription narcotics I could get a hold of. It soon turned to where I would go to several doctors in one week just so I could get my medications. I would take about 8 to 10 pills a day. I finally got "caught" by a doctor and he told me that I needed to quit. He gave me some Valium to help with the withdrawals. That seemed to help. I was able to quit the narcs for about 4 months until I had several large kidney stones. My doctor at the time gave me narcotics for the pain. The pain was so bad that I had to take them. Since my first round of kidney stones, I have had several more stones and about 5 surgeries to correct the problem. Now that my kidney stones are taken care of, I can't give up the pain pills.

I have been happily married for 7 years to a very loving wife. I have 2 wonderful children. My addiction now has gotten so bad that I am in fear of losing everything that I have, most importantly, my family. I have heard of a medication that can be given to help people like me. I am willing to do whatever it takes to cure myself and save my life. I just need a little help.

Thank you for your time,
Jason Behle

About twelve weeks after he passed and we received the autopsy reports, we learned that it wasn't only the sleep apnea and tonsillitis that killed him. Yes, it had played a role, but the main cause was the exact prescription his doctor had given him, the one that was supposed to help him with his cravings and save him from losing what matters most to him.

His body didn't break down the Methadone like it should have. He took the recommended amount, but his body held onto it and he was found to have a lethal amount and died that night while sleeping.

The thing he feared the most, losing his family, had happened.

10

"When you are going through difficulty and wonder where GOD is, remember the teacher is always quiet during the test." —Unknown source

In the last film of one of my favorite movie series, the main character Rocky is a retired boxing champ. He's aging and starts talking about coming out of retirement and wants a shot to fight again. His brother-in-law Paulie laughs as he thinks it's a ridiculous idea and says:

"What haven't you peaked yet?"

Rocky gets a little bit emotional as he says, "There's still some stuff in the basement," referring to the pain he feels after his wife passed away. He feels like there's this beast inside him and he needs to get it out.

I've realized that for years, I've had some stuff trapped deep down in my basement as well. Many of us do. We hold onto something in our past that is keeping us from reaching our true full potential. I know this is how it's been for me. I've been suppressing and hiding a beast rather than confronting and overcoming it.

This 'stuff in my basement' has tugged so strongly that it literally has caused me to doubt many things, but most importantly the faith I once thought was immovable. Things I was once certain of were now coming into serious questioning.

The word faith can be used in many ways and is often used when referring to a higher power or belief which is typically based on spiritual apprehension, rather than proof. It's a personal thing. It's a feeling, a testament of something you've received a witness to.

My faith and beliefs were what gave me the needed courage to serve as an ordained missionary at just nineteen years old. I had never lived away from home and was nervous to go away for two years to a third world foreign country, one full of poverty in the heart of South America. I had made the decision I wanted to go, despite the unknowing and I put my faith to the test that everything would be alright. I struggled, I grew, I served and had some wonderful experiences. I was tested greatly at times, but I knew it was just making it stronger with every obstacle that I endured and conquered.

Throughout my life, I've seen some pretty spiritual things happen. One of the most recent in my memory was back in 2010. My dad was diagnosed with stage four Melanoma cancer and was pretty much given a short death sentence. We believe that with help through the power of prayer he beat it then and has several times since these years. With experiences like this, why did I have serious doubts?

What about this basement stuff I'm talking about? What beast do I need to confront? Why did I start to question the things that I once knew and believed?

I was torn up inside. I wanted to be the best dad and husband possible for my family but knew my personal relationship with God was slipping away as I allowed a bitterness to fester and develop.

The chaos of life with two young kids, both of us juggling our careers, staying on top of finances and everything else in life was hectic. We worked it out so one of us was always able to be home with the kids. This has been a blessing for me. I've been able to spend a lot of time with them and I'll forever be grateful for this opportunity. Jena worked part time at the hospital, and I was able to get home early enough before she needed to leave for her shift.

Working as a nurse is something she loves, only her biggest dream in life has always been to be a mother and I've wanted to provide her the chance to stay home full time and be with the kids. Her shifts were long and strenuous, yet very fulfilling to her for the chance to serve others who are in need. I appreciated the time I got to be with my kids but felt bad that Jena worked these long shifts, even though she loves what she does.

This weighed on me. Even with us both working, things started getting tight financially. My business wasn't doing as well as in the past or what I had envisioned it would be doing at the time. We seemed to always just be getting by. We sold our boat and ended up going through quite a bit of savings during the months my business struggled to bring in more than just the expenses it took to run it.

Times have been tight before, but this year was different, harder. There didn't seem to be an easy solution that would work in our favor. We got insurance from my wife's employer, which is really good for hospital employees, so it seemed logical for her to keep working, only her part time turned into full time as I worked to keep the business alive and growing. We felt for our situation that one of us should be home with the kids, so me getting another job where I would be gone during the day didn't seem like the best solution at the time.

We've always had a great marriage. We have our little fights like everyone else; but it felt like they were happening more frequently at this time as the stress continued to pile on. I know everyone has struggles and ours are no worse than those of other people, it's just that all of these things added weight to the real problem I was dealing with. Actually, the majority of these things were most likely the result of how I was feeling and not handling "this beast in my basement." I let the bitterness consume me.

Have you ever noticed that when something goes wrong, we start looking for someone to blame? It's easier than accepting you might be the cause or dealing with the root of it. I started doing this with my creator and most things in my life and it put a large wedge in my relationship with him.

I remember sitting in church one Sunday morning and hearing a story from a lady who wanted to share how she knew God was listening and answers our prayers.

She explained how she was late getting the kids off to school and her to work because she could not find her car keys. She looked everywhere, under the couch, in the kitchen drawers, the car itself and of course her purse. Still nothing.

"Where could they be?" She asked while frantically searching every nook and cranny in her house.

After searching for twenty minutes or so she was getting frustrated with the situation. She realized she could either keep getting mad or ask God for some help. She dropped down to her knees with her children and they began to pray.

Her young child said the prayer and asked that the keys could be found so they could get to school and work. The moment she stood up, the mother looked over on the counter and peeking out from under some papers, she spotted the keys. She was sure she had already looked there, but sure enough there they were.

She mentioned how God didn't magically place her keys under the papers while they were asking for help, even though she believed he could have. He rather gave her the inspiration to look in the direction they were and to look closer than before.

Brad Behle

She testified on the power of prayer and that she knows he listens and hears us. Most importantly, he does answer us even when it's something as trivial as finding lost car keys.

Everyone in the congregation seemed so strengthened and moved by this story. Well, everyone but me. It actually did the opposite. It really bothered me. I don't think it was anything she said in particular; it was more the accumulation of all the similar stories I had heard during my lifetime about answered prayers.

In the Bible, the book of Matthew, there's a passage that says if you have faith, even as little as a mustard seed; it is enough to move mountains. Sounds pretty powerful right? Have a little faith and marvelous things can happen…?

I came to the point where I wondered why I had been trying the last thirty plus years to live a faithful life in the eyes of my creator. Why did I volunteer two years to serve a mission preaching his word and serving those in Paraguay, if I didn't really think he listens to us? Why strive to serve God if I didn't feel like he even listens or responds? Things I've asked about for years went unanswered. I've prayed, I've pleaded with him for help with issues I struggle with. When I questioned this to people who I thought were supposed to know the answers, I was told that I needed more faith and to ask God for answers.

"Jason, by the power of the priesthood, I command you to rise…if it be God's will." This prayer was offered by one of the most faithful men I knew, my own father.

This was actually a large part of the stuff deep down in my basement. I no longer believed God or that he truly intervened in our lives. I no longer felt like he was there for me or that he would help me with my own demons that I had consistently been praying to receive help with. We all have our demons and at times they seem too powerful to overcome on our own.

Sure, I had received plenty of signs in the past that should have helped me to not question my faith. God did heal the tumor on my brother's leg the doctors found after his skiing accident. Ironically though, it was this surgery that caused him to take the pain pills in the first place that ultimately ended up taking his life.

What miracle is there in the tumor disappearing if he ended up dying five years later after an intense struggle with an addiction? One that was started by the very surgery that was supposed to be a faith builder for us.

There is a lot of pain in the world. How does God choose who he does and doesn't bless? Everything I thought I knew in the past was now being shaken to the core.

I started seeing this dark side that I never focused on before. We all have a light and we're told that we need to let it shine unto the world. We all also have darkness. I unfortunately at the time was becoming more and more familiar with my own. I knew there was still good going on in the world, but why did all the bad seem to overshadow it? I felt horrible thinking like this. My life was good. I saw a bright light each day in my family but allowed the darkness to be more powerful. I tried to help other people and when I did, it numbed the pain temporarily, but I still felt broken inside.

I'd heard all the explanations before. I grew tired of all the typical answers I've always been told about just having "faith" that things will work out and that God has a plan. It's for our best. He loves us. Blah, blah, blah. This all seemed so shallow and more of a cop out, instead of really knowing the answers.

Yes, I know the struggles make us stronger. Working as a fitness trainer I understand this and realize that as we do strength training exercises, our muscles don't get stronger in that moment, they're actually being torn down. It's during the recovery that they rebuild and come back stronger, better than they were before.

Difficult things in life are placed to make us stronger. Overcoming spiritual obstacles strengthens our faith and we're better for it. I get it. I've heard it all before.

I'm not saying there shouldn't be hard things in life. They do make us develop into the best form of the person we can be. At this time in my life, I just found it silly to pray and ask for help, when I felt like we could handle things on our own. I felt I didn't need to pray to some all-powerful guy in the sky wondering if he even hears our cries for help or not. If he did hear them, did he even care? Or how could he possibly handle all the prayers coming in at once? There are a lot of problems in the world around us. It just seemed too fantasyland for me to believe anymore.

This was my new reality. It ate at me. It turned an optimistic, fun loving guy into someone that doubted things. I saw more of the negative side of life. I put on the front of being happy, but I was the opposite inside. I was mad as hell. I tried to combat it, I wanted to feel peace, it just seemed out of reach. I felt it needed to be found somewhere else other than with my previous belief of a loving heavenly being.

This was my sad new perspective.

My wife married a man she thought would be a faithful disciple of Christ and would raise his family on the same path they started on together. She deserved this. It bothered me that I was no longer this for her. I felt inadequate. I was failing her and the commitments I had made. I sadly even pondered if they would be better off without me, but knew I couldn't put my family through another loss. I didn't know how to fix this mess I was in.

I tried; well, I put on the image of trying. I still took the family to church every week and went through the motions, but I knew inside, as did Jena, that I had given up on what I had believed before.

I stopped praying for help or even to give gratitude. Sure, we gave thanks and asked to bless the food around the table at dinnertime, but I usually just had the kids say it so I wouldn't have to. I was just going through the motions.

The funny thing as I look back on this period of my life, is that I actually did continue doing something I started when I first got my bike. Each time I ride, I say a simple prayer asking for guidance and safety on the road. It must have been out of habit, but I still found myself saying a little prayer each time I got on the bike. Maybe there was still a little hope for me?

Even though I felt abandoned by God, and questioned and doubted him, I knew deep down there must still be something inside. Something buried deeper than that beast fighting to reach the surface.

I just needed to get it out and uncover the rest of the stuff in the basement in order to discover it again.

11

"Our greatest glory is not in never falling, but in rising every time we fall." —*Confucius*

Tyler had just arrived at my house to work out while the kids were down for a nap. We started doing some warmups to get the blood flowing and our muscles loosened up. The problem was, my mind wasn't there. I thought if I kept going, I would get into the zone and have a great workout. I'd forget what I was thinking about and could just focus on challenging myself physically.

I was wrong. I couldn't stop thinking of Keaton and his family. I knew I needed to pay them a visit right then at their house. They needed to know that a stranger was thinking of their son and ached for the pain they were enduring with his loss.

"Ty, hey man. I've got something I need to do. I learned about this young kid yesterday that died in a boating accident five months ago and my mind won't stop thinking about the family." I told him. "Cool if you stay here and get in your workout, while I go run something over to their house?"

"Yeah that's fine; I'll be here in case your kids wake from their naps but I need to get back to work in forty minutes, can you make it back by then?

"Yes, I'll hurry. Thanks man, I owe you," as I sprinted up my stairs.

I grabbed my phone and searched for their address online. I found it, but wasn't sure how recent it was and if they'd even be there in the middle of the afternoon. I didn't care. I needed to go try.

I remembered his obituary mentioned his love for reading books and that every morning he would wake up and bring down a different stuffed animal to name and play with for the day.

I knew I didn't have time to stop at the store and pick something up if I was going to make it back in time for my brother, so I ran up to my kids' playroom, knowing how spoiled the kids are by their grandmas and that their toy room is fully stocked.

I shuffled through some books and for the first time in a long time I said a silent little prayer. I asked to be guided in finding a book that would fit the situation and be meaningful to his family.

Just like the church lady and child who prayed to find the car keys, I knew my prayer was being answered as I immediately grabbed one I had never seen in their collection before. I read through it quickly, realizing I couldn't have picked a better one had I searched for hours at a bookstore.

I felt goosebumps across my body as I thought of what had just happened.

The book is written by Nancy Tillman and is titled *"On The Night You Were Born."*

I knew I would need to go get another copy in the next little while to read to my kids as I didn't even know we had this book. The funny thing is, a month later for Christmas, my mother-in-law happened to give the kids the same book as a gift. She didn't know we once had it and I had given it away to this special family. Was it a coincidence? I don't think so.

I found a container full of stuffed animals and grabbed one of the first I saw. It was a cute little monkey and it still had the new tag attached.

I threw some jeans on over my warm-ups knowing it was cold out. I then put on one of the only tangible things I have left from my brother, the leather riding jacket he got just months before he died.

I put on a beanie, strapped my helmet over it and went to the garage to warm up my Harley.

Here I was, all leathered up with a book and stuffed animal tucked inside my jacket and getting ready to ride to the house of a family I had never even met. The house was only fifteen minutes away from mine, so if I hustled, I could make it back in time for Ty to return to work. I pulled out of my neighborhood…

I had ridden down this road probably a hundred times before, only this time was different. I turned off of Redwood and onto Pioneer Crossing in Saratoga Springs, Utah. My mind was racing. I was confused about what I was doing and where I was heading, yet in my heart, I felt that my destination was inspired.

As I rode my Harley down the street, I had a feeling of complete calmness come over me. For the first time in a while, I knew I was going in the right direction. There was a peace surrounding me, one that had been familiar to me in the past, but which had been absent from my personal life for several years now. This time was different. This feeling was unlike any other I had ever felt before. It was purer than anything I had previously experienced. I was riding solo that day, but I knew for certain that I wasn't alone.

It was cold outside. I had on my leathers; still, the brisk late November air was especially chilly on my face. I had a decently long beard that I decided to grow out for the winter but I was now wishing it was even longer to protect my face from the bitterness of the early winter wind.

I was on my way to visit a family, one that I had never met and had only recently learned of the day before.

What was the purpose of riding over to their house on my Harley in the cold weather? At the time I didn't know the answer. I just knew that sometimes when you feel a strong urge to do a certain thing, especially when it feels like it's coming from someone or something bigger than yourself, you should probably go do it.

Cruising down the street, I wasn't really paying attention to the cold anymore. My mind was elsewhere, it was thinking of the things that have pushed me away for a while now, things that I kind of have kept hidden deep down inside. Then my mind started to ponder a word that has had a profound effect on me for the last ten years. What truly does the word *paradise* even mean? Is it a real place or just an imaginary location we make up to give us hope when we need a break from life?

"The Dictionary definition kept repeating in my head: 'a state of bliss, pure happiness or delight."

Each individual might have their own idea of what it is. Maybe to some it's the place you go after passing from this life and onto the next, a place where you are reunited with your creator and loved ones.

It could be a favorite place here on earth. One you can go to escape from all of your troubles to gain some clarity, away from the clutter of life. We all have our own description of what our personal paradise is.

To me, it's not one place in particular. It can be anywhere that you can find that blissful moment of pure happiness.

I often find this place when I'm on my motorcycle. I certainly found it on this particular cold day riding.

On my way to Keaton's parents' house, I said a simple prayer of gratitude for what was happening at that moment. I gave thanks for the immense love I was feeling, a feeling that was causing tears of joy to stream down my face as I rode. It felt as if a huge weight was being lifted off of my shoulders. I felt true love. I knew I wasn't alone. I was again riding with my brother and now his new little buddy, Keaton.

As I pulled up to the house, I knocked on the door. Keaton's mom Kimberli answered. Even though we had never met, I recognized her, as though in that moment, I knew her.

She looked at me and seemed a little surprised and perhaps confused. I imagine she wondered why a random biker in a black leather jacket and a big beard was standing at her doorstep.

"You're Keaton's mother, aren't you?" Her eyes lit up. "Yes, I am. How may I help you?"

"Ma'am, I am so sorry for the loss of your precious boy." I said.

"I learned of his story yesterday and haven't been able to stop thinking of your family since." I said, trying to hold back the tears. "I found his obituary online and read how he loved books and stuffed animals. I wanted to drop these off for you guys. I know that he's watching over all of you."

I gave her a hug and with tears in her eyes she whispered something I needed to hear.

"God Bless You."

This was one of the most powerful statements I had ever heard.

"He does bless me." The thought struck me like a bolt of lightning. Never before had this been clearer to me than in that exact moment.

He is real. I know this. I felt his presence that day. I felt my brother close by. I knew Keaton was thankful that I visited his mom and that they all guided me on this particular path. I will forever be grateful for what I felt and this experience.

God is different to many people. Whatever your belief in a higher power is, cherish it and know there is a purpose to our being here. It is not by chance.

In the Bible, in the book of Matthew, there's a passage that reads:

> *"Even as the Son of man came not to be ministered unto, but to minister, and give his life a ransom for many."*

I thought about this as I climbed on the Harley and started it up. I rode off slowly, hoping to never lose what I was feeling.

If Jesus, the only perfect among us, came to minister and serve others here on earth, shouldn't I? I realized that there is no greater calling, no better work to do than that of helping others. To be a servant. We all have opportunities to serve every day. What are we doing with them?

For the first time in ten years, as I cruised down the road, I finally had some clarity about something that had weighed extremely heavily on me for a long time. The unanswered prayer my father and I offered on behalf of my brother on that dreadful summer day. I wondered time and time again all these years why God didn't answer us and why my brother didn't rise? What is his will and why do we pray for things if he only does according only to his plan anyway?

I realized my brothers' mission here on earth was complete. I was assured of this while on the bike riding home.

A new perspective occurred to me for the first time. I thought of the possibility that when my dad commanded Jason to rise, maybe he wasn't meaning to reawaken on the hospital bed that day after all.

Maybe my dad's subconscious was more in tune than I was able to comprehend the last ten years. What if in a deeper sense my dad was telling him to rise and go be with God?

Maybe my father was given the chance to release his first-born son to return back home. Maybe God allowed this to happen so that my brother would feel at ease knowing his family would be okay without him for a while and that they would be taken care of.

"Rise" my father said… "If it be God's will."

Jason my son, return home with God, that is his will.

We are all limited to a certain amount of time here on this earth. Are we living it fully?

Will you be ready to rise and return home when your time comes?

I see things differently now than I did before this experience. Maybe "to rise" was also a message, a call to action to do more, to be more and to serve more. To rise up and be a better example for my kids. To rise up against my own demons.

Maybe our biggest accomplishment in life is in learning to get back up each time after falling.

A child doesn't stop trying to walk after falling again and again.

Our new little daughter, Preslee, took her first steps a couple months ago. This was a special moment for me, even though it meant it was time to baby proof the house and keep important things higher up and out of her reach. As she took 3–4 steps, we were all together as a family cheering her on. She fell down, we clapped and congratulated her, and she popped right back up with a big old smile on her face and tried walking again.

I couldn't help but think of falling in life and knowing how there is a cheering section encouraging us to continue, to get up and to try again. Maybe we don't hear them loudly, maybe they're a little more subtle, but I do believe they're there. They want the best for us.

Life will knock us down. We need to rise each time it does.

I don't have all the answers that I have searched for all these years. Truthfully, I'm not sure if I ever will, at least not in this life. I am learning to accept this.

I do know that as long as I continue to help other people, the bitterness fades away and I again feel the love I was so powerfully surrounded with on this ride.

That love I speak of is pure happiness.

It's said that God works in mysterious and wondrous ways. He knows what he's doing and has a plan. It's us that might not understand it and might see it as mysterious. But there is a purpose. More than ever, I realize that things happen the way they do for a reason. There is a bigger picture to all of this.

Since this inspired ride, I strive to keep finding families that are struggling and randomly showing up at their door with a handwritten note and a teddy bear. I'm still seeking that feeling from the first ride.

Several months after this experience with Keaton's family, I walked into my garage to get on my bike and noticed a new helmet sitting on the handlebars. It was blue and matched my bike. I immediately thought back to the original **Ride In Paradise** charity ride we had for my brother nearly ten years ago and how the logo we had made up was of a biker with a blue motorcycle wearing a matching blue helmet. My friend Jonathan didn't know anything about this ride or the logo with the matching helmet as he placed it on my bike to surprise me. I felt as if it were another sign that I am watched over and that I needed to continue doing these rides.

I like to think that I'm doing this out of straight charity for others and the goodness of my heart, but the truth is, it's more of a selfish reason. I long for that same feeling of peace and love. I often find it as I do these rides. I find it as I strive to do more for others, and I find it when I'm with my family striving to be the husband and father that my family deserves to have.

About six months after the ride, I again felt the now recognizable urge that I needed to reach back out to Keaton's family. I hand-wrote a letter to his parents hoping it would give them a little comfort to know that this experience had forever changed my life.

I was hesitant to share everything that I did in that letter. I told them of my many struggles and the reason I randomly showed up at their door on that cold November day. I wondered if they would remember me, as I knew that a lot of people had reached out to them since the accident. Would Kimberli recall the random bearded biker?

I again felt peace as I placed the letter in the box at the post office to be sent off.

About a week later my wife was on her way home from some delayed surgeries that made for a really long shift at work. She was worn out and wanted to just come in and crash.

Our mailbox is a couple blocks away and we usually pick it up once a week or so. Junk mail and bills don't inspire us to check the box all too often. As tired as she was, she decided to swing by and check to see if there was anything important. She walked into the house and placed the mail pile on the counter.

I went into the kitchen and looked through the stack. There in the middle was one addressed to me. It was from Kimberli. I felt calm as I picked it up and held it in my hand. I walked out on the front porch, opened it up and began to read.

It was dated July 6. Ten years to the day of my brother's passing. Coincidence? I don't believe so.

As I read it, a feeling of love surrounded my whole being. I wept as I reflected on the words she had written.

That day I showed up was a particularly hard one for her. Those days can come and go without warning. When she heard a knock on the door, she didn't want to answer it, but decided that she should.

I am grateful that she did.

It's said that God works in mysterious and wondrous ways and that his timing is perfect.

As she explained to her husband about the visitor she had earlier in the day and was wondering who it could have been, he was in awe. Unbeknownst to her, the night before he prayed deeply that she would find some form of peace and comfort in whatever way the Lord saw fit.

When she opened the door and saw me standing there, a biker dude in black leathers and a blue Harley Davidson, she knew her God was giving her a sign. He has a plan. He knows what he is doing.

She felt comfort as she thought of how the week before, she had surprised Scott with a brand-new Harley Davidson for his birthday. The wild thing about it, it also happened to be blue. She felt her son Keaton and God are watching over her and are mindful of her pain.

The Lord also knew that by having me call about that boat for sale, to learn of Keaton's accident and experience all that took place afterwards, would help me overcome the bitterness of the past and believe again in a higher purpose. He knew the open road on my bike was a language I could understand.

I am deeply grateful for this perfect moment. It has forever changed me.

Kimberli thought I was an angel on her doorstep that day, yet I felt that I rode to her house with two angels by my side that same day. Just as my brother has always looked out for me, I know he was once again as he and Keaton orchestrated this whole thing together. It was a way of letting us know that they are closer to us than we think.

I stood on the porch reading that letter. She said how happy she was for me that I could find peace and start to develop a relationship with my creator again. Knowing this helped immensely with the sting of her son's death.

It's said that he is a God of love. I felt his love reading that letter. I felt his love that cold November day on that ride. I felt Kimberli's love for me, a complete stranger in this life.

There is a purpose. There is a plan. I'm learning daily the importance of being in tune with this, so that I can continue to hear those subtle reminders.

I can make a difference in this life. I can make it a better world to live in for others, even by doing little things. You can as well, all of us can. Paradise is all around us. We are all connected.

This life is a journey. It has rolling hills, sharp turns and winding roads. When on it, enjoy it and don't be in a hurry because you are exactly where you need to be.

12

"For I am the Lord who heals you". —Exodus 15:26

JANUARY 2020.

It's been over six years since meeting Kimberli on her doorstep after learning about their little son, Keaton. A lot has happened in this time. Life is good. Jena and I added to our family and now have four kids. Bode, age 10; Solee, 8; Preslee, 5; and Hoven, 2. I closed down my fitness company several years ago and worked as an event director for three years. I was able to travel the country, putting on a 1000 ft slip-and-slide down city streets for a fun summer event. My wife, brothers, sister, mom and a couple friends joined my crew, so we traveled a couple of weekends a month during the summer. It was a blast and we were able to see different parts of the country. After the popularity of this event died, I took a job in business development as head of residential sales for a landscape construction company.

I'm still madly in love with my sweetheart, Jena and often wonder how I tricked her into marrying me over 15 years ago.

When I started writing this, it was so I would remember the timeline of everything, and it was a way to journal an experience that forever changed the direction of my life. As I put it all together and shared it with several people, they encouraged me to turn it into a book. I sent out the manuscript to a couple of publishers; it seemed to be well received, but none wanted to take a chance on a first-time author with a memoir.

I met a national publisher that works on a lot of Christian-themed books, and they were mildly interested. They help first time authors self-publish. We talked for a couple of months but the truth was, the timing never felt right for me to pursue it. It's a pretty personal story and I wasn't ready to put it out in public.

A couple of months ago, I started feeling like I needed to finish this and maybe by sharing, it could help strengthen another person's faith and they could see that if God touched a bearded biker's heart the way he did mine, he can touch anyone's.

I decided to take a drive out to Tooele, the city my brother and his family used to live in. I passed the hospital just off the main road and decided to go in. I've driven by it many times throughout the years, but the last time I stepped inside was the day Jason died there. Here I am, sitting in a chair in the same emergency room where I watched a doctor tell my parents their worst nightmare.

Sitting here, I feel peace. I can say with assurance that the Lord truly does heal. Sure, I still have questions and doubts, I still make a lot of mistakes, but the Lord knows and he loves me, just as he knows and loves you.

The last six years, I've been able to do a lot of teddy bear rides. One of my favorite things is riding down the street and having a car of kids honk and wave at me as I ride with a stuffed bear strapped to the back of my bike. Seeing their smiles always puts one on my face.

Through the years, I've realized this story isn't about me. It's about the families I've been blessed to meet at some of the darkest times in their lives. It's about an example of how the Lord knows each one of us individually and it's about finding our own path of healing and doing for others.

Though it's just a teddy bear and a handwritten note, these rides have changed my perspective on life. Each ride has its own experience and a feeling that will forever stay with me. Sometimes I've dropped the bear and note on the doorstep and ridden off, other times I've knocked on the door and given my condolences for their loss and quickly left, leaving them wondering who I was. Other times I've been invited inside the house and shared special moments with strangers that turn into friends.

One experience that really stands out to me is when I met Beau Richey's family. I learned from a friend about his tragic passing in a UTV accident. I saw how the family has such a positive attitude and the big influence this sixteen-year-old boy had on so many people. He loved the outdoors, motorcycles and his yellow Jeep with the license plate that read "Happi." He had a reminder set up on his phone a couple times a day that said "Make Christ the center of your life," reminding him to find someone to do an act of service for. There's a video online of a group of his friends singing one of his favorite songs for his family, "Rise Up" by Andra Day. When I watched it, I couldn't help but think of the influence these words have played in my life, like the prayer that I struggled with for years believing it hadn't been answered when my brother didn't rise up. But now these same words remind me to strive to be the best version of myself.

I knew I needed to pay a visit to this family. His mom, Liz, and his stepfather, Scott, lived about 30 minutes away from me, and his father David was only five to ten minutes away from them. I was excited, I could do two rides in one night.

I found two large teddy bears and wrote them letters. I hopped onto my bike one night after work. I arrived at his mom's house and as I was pulling up, his stepfather was taking the garbage out to the curb. I asked if this was Beau Richey's family. When he said it was, I mentioned I'd like to drop this off on the porch. He insisted that he go in and get Beau's mom and sister Ashley. They invited me inside. We talked for about an hour. It was great. I felt completely comfortable there and was amazed by their hospitality. When leaving, they gave me a yellow Live Like Beau wristband and a cool motorcycle vest his buddies made after he died that they wore to remember him. I left feeling inspired by this young boy and his family.

I then made my way to his dad's house. It was dark and getting late. I pulled up and he was outside as well, getting some groceries or something out of his car. We spoke for ten minutes before I rode off home. He asked my name. I'm usually hesitant as I've liked to be anonymous. I sign the card with "Ride In Paradise" rather than my name. The next day, David found me on Facebook and tagged me in a picture of the bear and shared how a stranger brought this on his Harley Davidson in memory of his late son, Beau. It felt good knowing it touched him.

Let's be honest, I'm a grown man giving teddy bears to other adults and their kids. It's not the manliest thing to do, but seeing when it means something to the families makes it worth it to me and motivates me to keep doing more.

Another time I came across a news article of a young girl named Natalie Petersen. She was riding a bike with a baby doll carrier on the back that looked so similar to the one we had given my daughter Solee just the month before. They were only a month apart in age so learning how she was tragically hit by a truck in her driveway, really shook me up.

My family and I made a four-hour trip down to southern Utah. We put my Harley and my son's electric motorcycle in a trailer and made a weekend trip out of it. We stayed at a hotel, swam in the pool and waited for the rain to clear so we could head over to surprise this wonderful family.

We strapped the largest teddy bear we could find on the back of my bike and my son, Bode and I rode through their neighborhood to their house, followed by Jena and our daughter, Solee. We all walked up to the door and knocked. I had arranged beforehand with a family member so they would be home. They invited us in. We talked about their daughter and learned more about her and took some pictures. Seeing the young siblings snuggle and wrestle the bear that was twice their size made the whole trip worth it.

Another time was for two guys I've looked up to for many years. They are brothers, Chad and Brian Hymas.

Chad was in an accident several years back and is now paralyzed from the chest down. He travels the world sharing and inspiring others. I actually grew up with his brother Brian. He was close friends with my brother Jason and between the two of us in age. He's been a great friend to me through the years. When I learned of their sister Bre's passing, I knew I wanted to do something for them.

Chad lives on a ranch about an hour away. I looked forward to the pretty ride out and there, and then would head north for about another hour to Brian's house. I knew they both had kids and thought they would enjoy the teddy bears.

I doorbell-ditched both, leaving the bears and notes on their doorsteps.

Not long after arriving home, I received a text from my parents who know Chad and admire his work. They sent me a screenshot of what Chad had posted on social media about the random act of kindness he received from a stranger on a Harley who rode up to his house, rang the doorbell and left a note with a bear. He said how this meant the world to him and that it was needed on a day that he was really struggling. I felt good knowing it touched him.

After 4-year-old Brighton Tenney unexpectedly passed away from an illness, her parents started an organization that gives back to others called Brighton A Day.

They spread the message of doing random acts of kindness for others as a way to cope with their loss and give back after so many rallied behind them when they were in need.

Showing up at their door with a teddy bear in hand made me smile and I prayed that it was a random act that brought a smile to them as well.

I've done rides for people I know and for complete strangers. When my grandfather, Papa passed away in 2014, I had my kids help me do a ride for both my grandmother Mum and my mom. They still have their bears on display at their homes and I hope it helps them think of Papa when they see it.

A couple of years back, when Jena's grandmother, Zola passed, my daughter and I surprised my mother-in-law

Cyndi with a bear to remember her mom. She has collected stuffed animals, so we were happy to add to the collection of one that hopefully helps her remember Grandma Zola.

I've tried to do at least one Ride In Paradise a month. During some of the warmer months I've done more, and fewer in the winter months when there is a lot of Utah snow.

About a year into doing these rides, my beard had grown really long. In fact, my two youngest kids have never known me with a clean, smooth face. There is a backstory and reason why I haven't been able to bring myself to shave off the beard just yet.

It started when my wife mentioned she thought it was time to have our third baby. I told her that getting pregnant is natural for a woman and as a guy it's natural to grow a beard. So, we should grow together: her a baby and me a beard. I had already grown a burly beard for six months; this was around the time I first met Kimberli as the big bearded biker that showed up at her door that bitter cold November day. A couple months later I regretfully shaved it off.

So, here was round two of the beard. I was excited for the new plan. Jena wasn't in the least but was a good sport about it. It was getting long and burly. Our daughter Preslee arrived and it was time for me to take it off, but then I thought, well I've gone ten months, I might as well keep going another two months and make the coveted "yeard" mark of a yearlong beard.

One day at a local home improvement store, I was standing in line to pay. I looked up and caught the eyes of a guy looking straight at me. He started to walk over. Still looking in his eyes, I could see a deep pain, but for a moment I saw a glimpse of happiness, as he smiled.

"Sorry to bother you," he said. "I just needed to come over and tell you how cool my son would think your beard is." He drowned a couple months ago. He always wanted me to grow a beard, so I'm growing this one out for him."

Wow. I was taken back. I shook his hand, asked his name and gave my condolences for his loss.

As I walked out of the store, I felt gratitude that he approached me and happy that a simple beard could give him a reminder of his son.

I knew what I needed to do. I feel so completely blessed that God gives me these subtle reminders to do something as trivial as a Ride In Paradise, but it's something I don't take lightly. I know others like this father are in pain and hope that I can bring a little light to their day, even for a small moment. Plus, I've already explained I do them for me and the selfish good vibes I feel.

There really isn't a timeframe to them. I do like to wait a couple of months after I learn of a death. I know for my family, the first couple of weeks we had so much support from so many, but after a while people understandably move on, yet the family is left with a gaping hole that doesn't seem to ever fill in. As time passes, I feel that it's kind of nice to get a random surprise down the road when that support isn't quite as constant.

I did a little research and found an article and the obituary of this gentleman's son. His name was Tucker Smith. He drowned while swimming at a reservoir in Hyrum, Utah.

I found the address of his parents' house. My son Bode, who was 6 at the time, and I loaded up on the motorcycle with a teddy bear and a handwritten note. I'm not sure how I'm doing as a father, but these last six years, I have involved all of my kids in several of these rides and I can only hope it helps instill a sense of service into their hearts.

Their house was about a twenty-minute ride away. While riding, I actually started having some doubts about going over. I thought of all that was going on in my life and some other stuff I needed to take care of. My dad recently was in a serious car accident that we learned was caused by a brain tumor; I had work, family and a million other things to get done. Sometimes I feel insecure doing these rides and wonder if they're worth the effort. Despite the many remarkable experiences, I've had, it's funny how my mind can play tricks and negative thoughts begin to flood in. It's true with so many things in life. There is always opposition, but we need to push through.

We arrived at their house to find it empty-looking, and it appeared that no one was living there. We decided to ride around the neighborhood and see if we could find someone that might know the family. We found a guy who said he knew the Smith's and that they had recently moved down the street. He then pointed us in the right direction.

They had a long gravel driveway and I could see several cars close to the house. We rode up, got off the bike and walked up with the bear. We knocked and waited for them to answer. They opened the door and I asked if this was the Smith residence.

They invited us in. I saw the parents, a couple kids and what seemed to be two guests dressed in Sunday best. Just then, one of the gentlemen hugged the father and I heard him softly say, "We sure miss you."

They looked at us and I apologized for interrupting. I handed the father the card and my son gave the mother the teddy bear.

"We're sorry for your loss. Tucker seemed like a great kid. We wanted to let you know that we're thinking of your family."

We got back on the bike and rode off. The feeling came back. The one I strive for. I was overwhelmed as I thought of meeting this father a couple months back at the hardware store and how I doubted he recognized me. I didn't know what the man meant when he whispered to the father, "We sure miss you." I imagined they were from the local church and I couldn't help but think that maybe they were referring to not seeing the family on Sunday service anymore. I thought about my own bitterness and the different ways I've dealt with it. This family has suffered the unimaginable.

Maybe the father had given up on God, just like I had two years before. Of course, I don't know their situation, their thoughts or what is going on in their life, but in the letter I told them how these rides make me feel closer to my brother and hopefully this bear and card could somehow let them feel closer to their son, even for a brief moment.

As we rode off, I realized we were where we needed to be that night. The doubtful thoughts of why I do this were gone. I was grateful to have crossed paths with this father several months back.

13

"Life Comes Full Circle"—Tracey Gold

A couple years into doing the Ride In Paradise, I was invited to speak at a conference in Boise, Idaho and share a little bit about the experience. I was excited to head up there and see my niece and nephew. After my brother's wife Michelle remarried, they moved up near Boise. With them being over five hours away, and part of a new family, many years we didn't see them more than once or twice a year. At the time of the conference, my niece Mykell was around sixteen and had sadly just lost a close friend to suicide. I thought it would be a good time for us to bond and drop off a bear to his family. Knowing I was driving and not riding my motorcycle up, I contacted the closest Harley Davidson dealership. After explaining my plans, they were so awesome and loaned me a Harley Road King for a couple of hours.

I spent the morning attending breakout sessions at the conference and during the lunch break, I went and picked my niece up on the bike and we delivered a teddy bear to Jacob's family. It was a cool experience to involve my niece in this and I smiled from ear to ear as we rode away. Since then, she's been able to do a couple more rides with me when she's been down in Utah.

When I started to present and looked out into the audience, I saw my wife, mom, grandmother Mum, my niece Mykell and her mother, Michelle. It was great to have the support and seeing my brother's ex-wife there was really good for me. Unfortunately, in years past, there were some bad feelings in both families and some drama that came with all the life changes and the process of trying to grieve. Seeing her there helped me finally put my own bitter feelings aside. Yeah, I lost my older brother, my faith had been shaken, it sucked, but I more recognized the pain she experienced. It was her husband that died. She's the one who found him and administered CPR to him while on the phone with 911. Her two kids lost their father and it was she who had to let them know that their father wasn't coming back home.

About a year ago, while out riding, a thought popped into my head. I was wearing my black leather jacket that I always do on a ride. It's one of the only things I have left from my brother, so it understandably has some strong sentimental value. The thought I had was one I was hesitant about. It was that I should give the jacket to his son, Luke. He was only two when his dad died so he doesn't have many memories of him other than what he's been told. I knew it would be special for him to have it as a keepsake of his dad.

I'll admit, I struggled and ignored this thought for a couple months. I finally called his mom and asked if it would be something, he would be interesting in having. She said he recently mentioned he wanted to get a leather jacket, so getting his father's would mean a lot.

I texted Luke that he had a surprise waiting for him the next time he came down to visit.

A couple of months later he came to stay the weekend with my parents. By this time, he was anxious and had already asked me multiple times about getting the surprise. The day he arrived, we decided to meet for lunch at grandma's house. It was a hot July, the middle of the summer Utah day. I arrived as they were pulling into the driveway, got out of my truck with the jacket and approached my nephew.

"Luke, I've had something that belonged to your Dad, Jas and it's meant a lot to me to have it, but I thought it would be really cool to pass it down to you. It's yours now. He'd want you to have it."

When I handed it to him, he had a blank expression on his face as he slipped his arms through the sleeves, put it over his shoulders and zipped it up. Tears then started to roll down his cheeks. It's 100 degrees outside and he's standing on the hot driveway wearing a black leather jacket. We hugged him and then stepped away to give him some time. He didn't move, just stood there with his new jacket on while he wept. I couldn't help but smile and feel grateful.

Over twenty years before, I was his dad's best man on his wedding day. Years later, his dad wasn't there for my wedding, so we dressed two-year-old Luke in a tuxedo, and he took his father's role as my best man.

As much as I struggled to give the jacket away, realistically I had just been its guardian for the last fifteen years. Now that Luke was older and could appreciate and wear it, it was clear that it belonged to him. Jason would want him to have it.

He just stood there, silently wearing his new jacket. I felt like a large part of my life had begun to complete a full circle.

A couple of months later I received a letter from Luke's mom Michelle. She thanked me for giving him the jacket and told me how one day she had a recurring thought to open a drawer she hadn't in a while. Right there on top was my brother's ambulance nametag that he wore every day and was so proud of. She thought he would want me to have it for giving Luke his jacket.

14

What's your Teddy Bear?

This past summer, I ran into Luke, a childhood friend, at a gas station. As we were catching up, I asked about his little nephew, Nixon. He was battling osteosarcoma and not doing well. Luke told me how Nixon was just put on hospice care and they didn't think he would be around much longer. Nixon's father, Nick, is a longtime buddy. We played high school football together years ago. He recently posted on social media that his son's life and battle were coming to an end now because the cancer had spread. Nixon's story had gone viral, touching the hearts of people all around the world. A healthy, strong, athletic six-year-old boy complained of growing pains that ended up being bone cancer. He fought hard for a year and a half. His leg was amputated, yet he learned to walk and even play sports again, inspiring all of us as we watched him.

For a while I have been considering starting my own line of teddy bears. I've been buying so many for these rides and could never really find one that fit the role of what I thought the bear should look like or what I imagined his personality to be.

All the bears I had found up to this point we're too cute and cuddly. I wanted a bear with a little more edge. One that stood for doing good for others, a "philantroplush," as I call it, unique and tough looking yet still kind and fun. I wanted to create a bear that I could give away during a Ride In Paradise, but also more than that. A bear that could do rad stuff like help raise money for different causes, inspire others to do cool things and most importantly, help people smile.

After hearing about Nixon's outlook, I knew I needed to act quickly. I wanted to plan something for him, a surprise to bring him a little happiness.

Unfortunately, Nixon passed away that night and it was a reminder to me of the importance of acting on impressions.

A couple months later, my son and I rode to the Whatcotts' house and walked up to their doorstep. We went inside, talked for a while and left them with three bears for their other kids, a note and a couple engraved #Nixonstrong watches from the Nixon Watch Company. They were touched by his story and kind enough to donate some watches. I left feeling grateful for the opportunity to do this ride with my son, for the attitude this family has after dealing with so much. I felt inspired to continue on with my gut feeling of doing these rides and creating something bigger than myself. Something that could give back in other ways and leave a mark on the world.

Have you ever heard the term USP? It's used often in sales and is the abbreviation for Unique *Selling* Proposition. It's what sets you apart from others, the reason

someone would want what you're offering rather than what someone else has. What makes what you're offering unique?

Let's switch it around a little bit and swap the "selling" for "service". What is your USP—your Unique *Service* Proposition?

In what way can you serve? How can you uniquely help others in a way better than anyone else? How can you make the world a little bit better in your own special way?

I know a lot of people have served and helped me. Even with this ride. My good friend Coby owns a graphic and sign shop. He had his team design a logo and wrapped it on my gas tank. He wouldn't ever let me pay him. This has meant a lot to me through the years.

I mentioned how I always sign the card with "Ride In Paradise" rather than my name. A couple years back, I wanted to create a video that gave an idea of what it was about, and I also considered making this into a charity organization. I decided to keep it small and more personal. A friend of mine named Jared, who creates professional films, flew out from North Carolina and helped tell the story of the ride. Scott, Kimberli, some other friends, my brother Ty, his wife Chelle and daughter Brixy all acted in the film and gave of their time.

I truly believe a key to a happy life is to give. To "give yourself" and to "give of yourself."

What do I mean by giving yourself? I'm talking about allowing yourself time for self-care. Do things that you enjoy, things that excite you, that get the blood pumping and make you feel alive. I would be a mental mess if I didn't take time to exercise and do other things that I am passionate about. The fun thing is that many of these things I'm able to do with my wife and kids.

Look, I get it, we're all busy. Finding self-time is hard and can seem selfish. It's not. Make it a priority. I've found it helps me tremendously in my life. I show up as a better husband, father, son, brother and friend.

Now, if there is anything, I've learned these past six years, it's the power in giving of yourself.

Whenever I find myself in a funk and weighed down by life, it's often because I'm not actively doing for others as much as I should be. I quickly try to change that and I am usually amazed with the sudden mood change that happens by serving.

Some might think the Ride In Paradise seems depressing and focuses a lot on death. I think of it as the opposite. It helps me remember how blessed I am to wake each day. Not everyone gets to. Yesterday was the last day on earth for hundreds of thousands of people. Do you realize YOU WOKE UP, TODAY? You've been given another chance, a blank slate. You have dreams to fulfill! You have

God-given talents and gifts that he wants you to share with the world.

As random as my USP is, I'm motivated now more than ever to give in my own unique way. I want to give more and more teddy bears away. They always make someone smile, no matter the age.

I've realized and have experienced personally that sometimes we need to know the darkness before we can truly appreciate the light. And there seems to be a lot of darkness in the world right now. We all have monsters we're fighting, stuff that we're dealing with. Remember though, the sun always rises after the night and lights up the sky. Without the darkness, there would be no light.

There's so much good out there. When learning to ride motorcycles, you're taught that you go where you look, so pay attention to the direction you're heading. As in life, we see what we want to see. Look for the good and be part of the good.

We are all meant to shine, to be a light to the world. Let's stop feeling insecure. We're all in this together. Doing the Ride In Paradise is a shining light for me and I plan to continue doing it as long as the good Lord allows me to be here on this earth.

Sharing this story is something I've been unsure about. I still deal with doubts and have questions. I'm far from perfect and I can be a knucklehead at times, but I do know

I'm loved and so are you. I hope as I share this, it will help others shine a little brighter.

As I write this, I'm listening to "I can only imagine" by MercyMe. This song has been a huge source of inspiration to myself and my family throughout the years.

Go find your light. Find what your "Teddy Bear" is and proudly share it with others.

I can only imagine how much better things can be, if we all go and do this.

"We know we're coming full circle with God when we stand at a very similar crossroad where we made such a mess of life before, but this time we take a different road."

—Beth Moore

15

I command you to Rise...if it be God's will.
—Fred Behle

MARCH 3, 2021.

Today we laid my father, Fred Behle down to rest. He battled cancer for 11 years, 7 of which we never thought we would have. Doctors and the statistics said he wouldn't live this long. I'm grateful he did.

He passed peacefully on February 25, 2021, with his sweetheart of 44 years by his side.

The last month has been one of the most tender times of my life. I've been able to serve my dad in ways I will never forget. Watching my mom be so compassionate and loving to him has been so inspiring to see.

Several weeks ago, I was at my parents' house helping my friend, Justin Vanderlinden install a kitchen backsplash. At this point, my dad didn't get around very well and had to use a walker.

We were in the garage putting away the tools and talking with my mom when we heard him cry "Debbie". We ran inside and found him on the ground. He had tried to get up off the couch and lost his balance. He hit his head on the fireplace tile and cut his eyebrow.

As we reached our arms under his and began lifting, I couldn't help but think of the blessing he gave my brother so many years ago when he commanded him to 'rise'.

I was overtaken with emotion. I felt humbled with the opportunity to help my father in that moment after all he has done for me.

The next couple of weeks he quickly declined. With tumors all over his body, we could only try and keep him comfortable. Several times a day, we lifted him from his hospital bed to the wheelchair and then back into the bed. I will forever cherish these under the arm, chest to chest 'bear hugs' it took to move him.

Jena recently pointed out to me that for 7 years I have delivered teddy bears to others with the hope of helping them find some comfort and how ironic that I have found so much comfort of my own in giving and receiving these 'bear hugs' with my dad the last few weeks. Just before closing the casket, I placed a mini bear wearing a University of Utah bandana next to him in honor of these hugs and all the times watching his favorite team with him and my brothers.

Four days before he passed, we gathered together as a family. We had fasted and prayed during the day that he would be comfortable and peaceful with his time left.

Me, Mike, Ty and our brother-in-law, Jordan placed our hands on our father's head to give him a blessing. I could feel the presence of Jason nearby.

I prayed that when the Lord called Dad home, he would 'rise' up.

After all these years, I'm beginning to understand the lesson my dad taught me about being in line with God's will and that things take place on his timeline, not ours.

I will strive to be the father to my kids that my dad was to me. He is simply, the greatest man I've ever known.

As much as I will miss him, the thought of him and his oldest son embracing after all these years puts a smile on my face.

It took me a long time to find peace with Jason's passing. I get nervous I will forget all that I've learned and have experienced the past several years as these feelings of grief resurface but for now, I feel at peace.

"I command you to rise."

Dad, I promise I will each time that I fall. I promise to help others do the same. I'll be there for mom, like you asked me to be.

I am finally ready to share this story. I feel it has now completed a full circle. I am honored to finish it with your last chapter here on earth. Thank you for everything, Dad.

Luke 15:20 (KJV)

"And he arose and came to his father. But when he was yet a great way off, his father saw him, and had compassion, and ran, and fell on his neck, and kissed him."

I love ya, Pops. I'll miss you. Watch over us just as I know Jason is. Oh, and while you're at it, please give him a big bear hug for me.

AFTERWORD

I was having a bad day. It seemed like all of the days were that way, since the death of our 5-year-old son. It had only been about 5 months, and I could not see the light. The physicality of the ache was unrelenting. I had no energy, nor will, for that matter, to interact with the outside world. Unbeknownst to me, my husband, just that morning, had helplessly pleaded with God to please send some relief to me.

I was folding laundry when there was a knock on the door. I wasn't really answering the door at that point, but I looked outside and saw a blue Harley parked at the curb. It was the exact same color of my husband's Harley. I felt compelled to see who it was, and I answered the door to a heavily bearded Stranger, dressed top to bottom in black leather riding gear.

"Are you Keaton's mom?" he asked me.

I took a step back from the door, a little bit wary, and answered, "Yes…"

He briefly told me the story of calling on a boat that was for sale. He asked our son-in-law, Aaron, why he was selling the boat. Aaron, who is generally a very private person, told the Stranger about the experience of losing our son in a boating accident at Lake Powell.

"I just wanted to tell you that I am so sorry for your loss," said the Stranger, as he handed me a book and a stuffed monkey. He then asked if he could give me a hug.

With tears in my eyes, I accepted the hug as I uttered, "God bless you."

He had simply signed the book from "The Do-Good Biker Dude."

I cannot describe the feeling of love and respite that that interaction brought me and my family. I was known by God, and He had sent this angel to convey His love for me.

Months later, we received a letter from The Do-Good Biker dude. We were thrilled, as his identity had been a total mystery to us. He related the story of losing his brother, and his faith. We were overwhelmed and so grateful that our angel had a name, and that we could finally share with him what he meant to us.

Fast forward 7 years, and to this day, Brad is still our angel, and a dear, dear friend. I am so grateful that he listened to the whisperings of his brother and the Spirit that day. It changed me forever.

I am grateful to Brad for opening up and sharing his journey. You too are known by a loving God who is aware of all that you are experiencing.

—Kimberli Howard

Made in the USA
Columbia, SC
21 July 2021